Why You Will Love *Inner Power Now*

Anita Moorjani – Bestselling Author and Speaker

A book for all ages, Inner Power Now *uses exercises, visualization and guided imagery techniques to empower and stimulate the healing responses in the body to achieve mental and physical well-being. User friendly, and equipped with valuable tools this book will support you on your healing journey.*

–**Anita Moorjani,** *New York Times* **best-selling Author of** *Dying to be Me* **and** *What if This is Heaven.*

James Baraz – Mindfulness Leader and Author

"What a wonderful contribution! Besides good medical care, parents, caregivers and children, facing a child's serious health challenge, need all the emotional support they can get. With Inner Power Now *they can realize the most important resource for that support is right inside themselves. The guided imagery they learn can help support genuine healing. But even more, they can transform an attitude of «helpless victim» into a one of active participant of self-care, giving a profound feeling of empowerment. With warmth, encouragement and skillfulness Vicki Atlas Israel has written an important guidebook for navigating a difficult journey. Well done!"*

–**James Baraz, co-author of** *Awakening Joy* **and** *Awakening Joy for Kids***;
co-founding teacher Spirit Rock Meditation Center, Woodacre, California**

Judy Fisher-Sadoff, Former Client

My mom was living with us and although her mantra was "don't get old"—aging was inevitable. Our roles reversed. I became her caregiver. It was hard, but I put my heart and soul into her care...so did my young daughter. After ten years-plus of structuring my world around moms— the emotional and physical stress, constant logistics was taking a toll on me. I felt my daughter and I would benefit greatly from weekly sessions with Vick—so, we started the program from "Stress to Inner Peace." I immediately felt connected to Vicki.

My daughter and I learned to use our mind to calm down, deflect unhealthy stress, meditate, develop our focus for homework & home life. It was wonderful, memorable quality time with my teenager. Vicki is a special person. She answered this unexpected call and has begun the most worthwhile endeavor. I'm a believer. The meditations and guided imagery she provides is vital to our emotional, spiritual and physical health and that of our children. The Millennials will need these tools, visualizations, tapping into the power of the imagination, more than ever.

My mother passed away recently. I am so grateful for the days and golden years spent with her. No regrets. Only love.

Thank you, Vicki.

With love,

–**Judy Fisher-Sadoff**
Parent and Family Client

Sandy Jost – Author and Educator Guided Imagery

Vicki Atlas-Israel was an intensely dedicated student of mine for years, but it didn't take me long at all to realize that she had the perfect tools to be extraordinary at making this her life's work. Vicki's communication skills alone are exceptional, but her VOICE is blessed with a resonance that will allow you to hear directly from her heart!

Inner Power Now has emerged from Vicki's passion to help parents and their children through the most turbulent of life's storms. She knows. She cares. And her own life experiences prepared her perfectly to provide you with some help.

Vicki puts quality behind everything she does, which is why she is so highly respected in the entire media industry. Let her words soothe you now as you seek answers to questions that you may not even currently believe have an answer.

The beauty of this book is that you can get outside of your own story and…fall in love with "Lucy the Lama"…learn to "breathe like a Navy Seal"…and allow shared anecdotes to convince you…that there is indeed hope for your own personal situation.

This is exactly what Vicki's book will enable you to do… speak to the deepest parts of yourself that are actually seeking to be healed. When you trust in this process, only then can the magic truly begin.

–Sandy Jost, PhD
Author and Educator
ONE Health Academy Integrative Medicine
www.HealingImages.com

INNER POWER
now

Healing Meditations to Reduce Stress and Pain so Children and Families Thrive

VICKI ATLAS ISRAEL

Inner Power Now
Healing Meditations to Reduce Stress and Pain so Children and Families Thrive
Vicki Atlas Israel
Inner Power Mindset

Published by Inner Power Mindset
Copyright ©2019 Vicki Atlas Israel
All rights reserved.

No part of this publication may be reproduced, stored in a retrieval system, or transmitted in any form or by any means, electronic, mechanical, photocopying, recording, scanning, or otherwise, except as permitted under Section 107 or 108 of the 1976 United States Copyright Act, without the prior written permission of the Publisher. Requests to the Publisher for permission should be addressed to Permissions Department, Inner Power Mindset, info@InnerPowerMindset.com.

Limit of Liability/Disclaimer of Warranty: While the publisher and author have used their best efforts in preparing this book, they make no representations or warranties with respect to the accuracy or completeness of the contents of this book and specifically disclaim any implied warranties of merchantability or fitness for a particular purpose. No warranty may be created or extended by sales representatives or written sales materials. The advice and strategies contained herein may not be suitable for your situation. You should consult with a professional where appropriate. Neither the publisher nor author shall be liable for any loss of profit or any other commercial damages, including but not limited to special, incidental, consequential, or other damages.

Editor: Lisbeth Tanz, FuzzyDogLLC.com

Illustrator: Catharine Magel, catharinemagelpa.com

Cover and Interior design: Davis Creative, DavisCreative.com

Publisher's Cataloging-In-Publication Data
(Prepared by The Donohue Group, Inc.)

Names: Israel, Vicki Atlas, author. | Magel, Catharine, illustrator.

Title: Inner power now : healing meditations to reduce stress and pain so children and families thrive / Vicki Atlas Israel ; [illustrator: Catharine Magel].

Description: [St. Louis, Missouri] : Inner Power Mindset, [2019] | Includes bibliographical references.

Identifiers: ISBN 9781733715201 | ISBN 9781733715218 (ebook)

Subjects: LCSH: Meditations. | Stress management. | Mindfulness (Psychology) | Families--Psychological aspects. | Adolescent psychology. | Sick children--Mental health. | BISAC: FAMILY & RELATIONSHIPS / Life Stages / School Age. | PSYCHOLOGY / Developmental / Adolescent. | BODY, MIND & SPIRIT / Mindfulness & Meditation.

Classification: LCC BF637.M4 I87 2019 (print) | LCC BF637.M4 (ebook) | DDC 158.12--dc23 2019

ATTENTION CORPORATIONS, UNIVERSITIES, COLLEGES AND PROFESSIONAL ORGANIZATIONS: Quantity discounts are available on bulk purchases of this book for educational, gift purposes, or as premiums for increasing magazine subscriptions or renewals. Special books or book excerpts can also be created to fit specific needs. For information, please contact Inner Power Mindset, info@InnerPowerMindset.com.

Dedication

This book is dedicated to the families and clients that I have worked with over the years. You inspire and teach more than you will ever know! This book is also dedicated to parents who have a child or teen facing a serious illness or other life challenge. You and your children's health and happiness are what drives me to bring you the best resources and information.

I want to pay special tribute to New York Times Bestselling Author Jack Canfield and Co-creator of *Chicken Soup for the Soul* series. Jack, your generosity and gracious spirit has touched me deeply—first by writing a beautiful foreword for this book and then providing a special video message.

This book also is dedicated to my amazing and supportive family. I want to thank my generous and loving husband Jim, who has encouraged my dreams. I appreciate my sons, Andrew and Jonathan, for growing into amazing adults and being my very best teachers.

I'm very grateful to my dear sisters for their love, generosity, and encouragement: Laura Schlesinger, Patti Howe, and Marilyn Atlas Needham and my brothers-in-law Howard Schlesinger and Scott Needham, plus my beautiful extended family and friends. I appreciate the special illustrations for my book created by talented artist, Catharine Magel.

Special thanks go to cousins Al and Nancy Malnik who gave a donation to help launch this book and the *Inner Power NOW* program.

continued

Finally, I dedicate this book to my beautiful late mother, Annadine Krachmalnick Jaffee, who taught us how to be strong, loving, and giving, and to make a difference in the lives of others.

Table of Contents

Foreword — vii
Preface — ix
Introduction — 1

Part 1
For Parents, Caregivers, and Those Who Work with Children
Chapter 1: Inner Power NOW for Healing — 11
Chapter 2: The Power of Thoughts — 25
Chapter 3: Unleash Your Imagination — 39

Part 2
For Children and Teens
Chapter 4 Your Safe Place to Heal for Children and Teens — 51
Chapter 5: Meeting Your Inner Guide or Magical Wizard — 63
Chapter 6 : Tuning into Your Heart Star — 71
Chapter 7: Superpower Healing to Reduce Pain — 79
Chapter 8: Sleepytime Dreams for Children — 93

Part 3
For Teens, Parents, and Caregivers
Chapter 9: Inner Power NOW for Teens — 103
Chapter 10: Inner Power NOW for Parents and Caregivers — 123
Chapter 11: Your Healing Journey Continues — 141

Special Note to *Inner Power NOW* Readers — 155
Acknowledgments — 157
Endnotes — 161
About the Author — 165

Foreword

During one of my *Breakthrough to Success* Trainings, I heard Vicki speak about her book to help stressed out parents and children at pediatric hospitals and schools. I immediately knew this could be a beneficial resource to families. Right after she spoke, I joined her on stage and asked if I could endorse her book once it was done.

Now, here you hold the book in your hands—completed and packaged to help parents, children, teens, and caregivers. *Inner Power NOW* takes the mystery out of how to use meditation, mindfulness, and guided imagery for stress relief and healing. Included are helpful exercises, brief meditations, and guided imagery scripts that are easy to use. And Vicki also gives you access to free audio programs and more that go with the book.

Psychologists and doctors are just beginning to understand the awesome power of our mind/body connection. Over the past decade, thousands of research studies have proven that meditation, mindfulness, and guided imagery not only are successful in addressing stress-related illnesses, but also so much more. These techniques can provide healing before and after surgery and cancer treatments, and they can help with anxiety, depression, and sleep. There have also been studies with children showing how guided imagery benefits kids with chronic stomach pain, surgery, diabetes and Attention Deficit Disorder. With teens, research shows that embracing a mindfulness practice can help with school focus, self-esteem, and building relations.

I have personally witnessed the power of meditation, visualization and guided imagery in my work with hundreds of thousands of people around the world as well as in my personal and professional life. I taught all of my children how to meditate and use visualization to de-stress themselves both at school and in social situations. I also have benefited professionally from the practice of meditation. In fact, it was during one of my meditations that I received the title for my #1 New York Times best-selling book series—*Chicken Soup for the Soul*®.

You have probably picked up this book because of a serious illness or health challenge facing your child or a child you work with. I promise you that *Inner Power NOW* will make a difference and help you and your child thrive. Everyone will benefit from using these techniques to release stress and facilitate healing and happiness.

Wishing you and your children the best!

Jack Canfield
America's #1 Success Coach
CEO, The Canfield Training Group
Co-creator of *Chicken Soup for the Soul*®

Preface

One of the great miracles of the human body is its natural ability to heal. A skinned knee, a broken arm, and a winter cold can all be healed by our miraculous bodies. Scientists at the Smithsonian Institute now estimate we have thirty-seven trillion cells in the human body that know what to do and when to do it. But when something goes wrong, as when a chronic or life-threatening illness strikes, the body often needs help to heal. When the stricken person is a child, the parents and other family members often feel helpless and unsure of how to manage the situation and their emotions, not to mention how best to serve the ill child. I've written this book to help families navigate what can be rocky terrain through the use of breathing techniques, guided imagery, and other mindful tools.

You may not realize it, but within you, there's an inner coach and higher self that you may call upon at any time. Through guided imagery and using your imagination, you may embrace this inner guide for answers and healing. Mental imagery works by giving you healing imagery and positive feelings that stimulate the body's natural ability to heal. All you have to do is allow the process to lead you into a very relaxed state so the healing can begin. In the past two decades, hundreds of studies involving children and adults have proven the benefits of using guided imagery and meditation to calm anxiety and to heal faster.

Guided Imagery is a complementary healing practice that works alongside traditional medical care. As you go on these healing journeys together with your child, you'll both begin to feel more empowered and better equipped to manage the ongoing health challenges and everyday stresses of life. Working with your inner healer is a form of love and self-healing and brings with it an invitation to overcome the shame of being sick. The deeper you go into your guided imagery practice, allows you to awaken a loving compassion for yourself and others, while feeling more connected to a loving source.

The American Academy of Pediatrics estimates that there are between fifteen to eighteen million children who suffer from chronic health conditions. That's one out of every four children in the United States. There are also millions of families facing a mental health challenge with a child or teen, as suicide remains a leading cause of death among teens. Why not use all the power you possess and tap into this inner healer for stress relief, healing, pain control, and anxiety reduction? Plus, you will be feeling more love and peace.

As a Certified Guided Imagery Specialist and Best Mindset Coach, my goal is to make these guided imagery programs easily accessible and to give the greatest source of healing, stress relief, and empowerment possible. To make it easy, you'll find pre-recorded guided imagery audio and video programs on this book's companion website, where you'll also find a special gift at InnerPowerMindset.com/IPNgift

I am also excited to share that a team of researchers at a leading pediatric hospital and major university are studying the use of my guided imagery programs, breathing techniques, and coaching to help alleviate anxiety and pain.

Wishing you peace and many blessings,
Vick

Introduction

If you had told me nearly 10 years ago that I would be teaching other people how to awaken their inner power for more healing, happiness, and peace, I would have laughed. Stressed-out, anxious Vicki? The woman who has suffered from insomnia for years? I'm teaching others how to awaken love and healing? How is that possible, especially coming from a long line of worriers? I think it's in our family genes!

I'm grateful there was some spark that led me back to meditation and guided imagery ten years ago. These tools helped me to gradually turn my life around. Instead of feeling angst in the pit of my stomach, and constantly being in stress-mode, I was able to feel more at peace. It helped me reduce my anxiety, sleepless nights, and provided me with a more calm throughout my day. Now I want you, your children, and others to discover this amazing inner light of healing.

Sometimes it may be at our lowest point in life that we turn to something higher. That is what happened to me, my work, and this book. It's been a soul's journey of creation. Has it been all beautiful and flowing since waking up? The answer is no, not always. I still continue to wrestle with my lower self and ego at times. Sometimes I may feel totally overwhelmed, but it does not last as long. When I remember to accept what is, let in the light, and have faith, I can smile and be more of service to others.

There's a loving presence within each of us. When we wake up to this truth, we realize that we are co-creators. We can impact our life in more positive ways. The images that we see in our minds and the words that we use—they affect our experiences. Why not picture images of more healing and wholeness and the life that you want to create? Picture it vividly with all five senses and feel the joy of this vision happening now. With words, give yourself and your children more praise, instead of criticism. Teach your children and teens that they are lovable and they "are enough," just as they are.

As you enhance your happiness and resilience, you also affect your children's emotional wellbeing in a positive way. New research studies show that when parents engage in meditation, guided imagery and other mindfulness practices, they may improve the wellbeing of *others* in their lives—especially their children. The beauty is that you also will be strengthening your family bond.

Today, I am a Certified Guided Imagery Practitioner through ONE Health Academy of Integrative Medicine (HealingImages.com) and a Best Mindset Coach. I've been trained by Jack Canfield, Bestselling Author and Co-creator of *Chicken Soup for the Soul* Series® and co-author of the *Success Principles.*® He credits much of his success with utilizing meditation and visualization. I've also completed mindfulness retreats with James Baraz, author of *Awakening Joy.*

You may be familiar with Dr. Joe Dispenza, a neuroscience researcher, chiropractor, and best-selling author featured in the movie *What the Bleep Do We Know?!* I have attended his Progressive and Advanced Meditation Training. In his book, *Becoming Supernatural,* Dispenza discusses several incredible transformations by attendees at his advanced meditation workshops. Using brain scan technology, Dispenza, along with other neuroscientists, have captured images of participants' brains showing what happens before, during, and after group meditations. The results are fascinating. This research suggests we have access to an amazing energy field that everyday people can tap into for healing.

Guided Imagery (also known as creative visualization) is a powerful, yet gentle technique that focuses and directs the imagination in helpful ways. More than just visualizing, it's a multisensory experience with feelings intended to bring the body and mind's innate healing wisdom into more conscious awareness. According to numerous studies, imagery and meditation can enhance healing and overall well-being by putting positive imagery into your deeper subconscious mind. It provides benefits for adults and children.

My family will vouch for me; they see a difference, and they like the calmer me. In fact, I became a Certified Guided Imagery Practitioner several years ago, so I could help others tune into this healing, enjoy more ease, and empower their best life. Through this book, I'm sharing these wonderful mind-body tools to spread more love and healing.

Believe me. I get it. You may think your life is too stressful and overwhelming to tune into stillness or guided imagery. Time is a precious commodity, especially if you and your family are experiencing a health crisis. Yet, this is the perfect time to begin because it will provide stress relief, healing, and strength as well as give comfort. Plus, we offer several exercises that are only a few minutes to do in the beginning.

I have designed this book to be used by you and your child or teen. You might feel a bit silly at first. That's normal! Let go of judgment and put into practice these ancient spiritual practices that may really benefit your body, mind, and spirit. *You* are each a superhero, endowed with qualities from the Divine. It's truly possible for you to tap into your inner wisdom at any time. It's just a matter of letting go of the endless mental chatter to unleash your *Inner Power NOW!*

Explanation About This Book

This book is divided into three parts. Part One is for parents, therapists, healthcare providers, and educators who work with children. It describes the latest research, studies, and stories as to why and how breathing techniques, guided imagery, and meditation can aid healing.

Part Two is geared for children and teens. This section is more playful and introduces a loveable character, Lucy the Llama. I suggest you read the stories and exercises to your child first and then share the exercises together as a family. Part Three features more guided imagery especially for teens, parents, and caregivers.

Lucy the Llama

At any time, you may skip to the fun exercises and imagery tools. For example, the breathing techniques begin at the end of Chapter 1. The child's section begins with Chapter 4, which also includes a message to teens.

To make these exercises and guided imagery easy, you have access to recordings, so you can simply relax and listen. Using the recordings allows you to gain the most benefit of the guided imagery scripts because it becomes a multisensory experience. By listening to each guided imagery, any concerns about doing or saying it right is eliminated. Instead, you can relax and let the audio program work its healing magic.

The recordings can be found on this companion website. Go to InnerPowerMindset.com/IPNgift to experience your free trial.

A Special Note to Parents:

How can I begin to understand the heaviness in your heart? It can be so difficult to see a child suffer, especially your own. Being a parent myself, I can recall that moment—one of joy and of being overwhelmed when my first child was born. I remember thinking, "Wow, now I'm responsible for this tiny, human being. What if I mess up?" Although frightening and magical at the same time, we both know we would do anything for our child.

Having sons with chronic health conditions, I understand a little of what you may be facing. One son was diagnosed with attention deficit disorder (ADD); the other was thought to be on the autism spectrum but was later diagnosed with attention deficit hyperactivity disorder (ADHD) as well as asthma. Both have experienced physical, emotional, and social challenges.

You may feel uncertain and overwhelmed at times. I know I sure did. Please know that you're not to blame for your child's disease, chronic health condition, or illness. Honor your feelings. Hopefully, you will allow a power greater than yourself to help you through these challenging times. One thing you can do is to take one breath, and then another breath. Do what you need to do to take care of you, so that you are better able to help your precious child. That's how real comfort and healing will take place for you and your family. You will come through this together.

My gift to you is to offer support and to give you tools to relieve suffering and stress. For a few minutes a day, or whenever you have time, go inside yourself for a little peace and calm. You and your child will be able to experience the fun games and guided imagery journeys together. Some are very short, some are five minutes, and some are a little longer. My aim is to provide comfort and healing.

A recent study conducted in hospitals found parents feel out-of-control with more stress and anxiety when they don't know what to do to help their child. Using the tools in this book will help you feel more in control and be an aid in supporting your child's healing.

Please know this. You are the one with this inner power that is connected to All-That-Is, a power greater than yourself. Some call this God, Source, Spirit, or Universal Power. Whatever that is, you are the one that will bring healing to yourself and others, not me. Being still and listening to guided imagery is meant to relieve suffering and hold you up to the light. Sharing this time is such a gift and doing these visualizations together with your child may help build a stronger bond. I love your beautiful willingness to try. It's no accident that you found this book at this time.

Introduction

To Health Care Providers, Therapists, and Child Life Specialists

You are the bright star and leader to help your patient, families, and caregivers. By sharing this book with families, you will help them discover a holistic way to relieve pain and suffering. You will help them uncover a powerful love and light that connects them to their inner healer.

Do not doubt your part in this spark of loving care to bring comfort and relief. You hold magic in your hands as well as a beautiful compassion and hope for this family and child. If you are suffering from stress or discomfort, you won't be as available to those patients and families who need you most. Please feel free to also use these meditations and tools for your own health and happiness. By being more aware of a loving, calming presence within your heart, you will bring more comfort to those in need.

Part 1

For Parents, Caregivers, and Those Who Work with Children

CHAPTER 1

Inner Power NOW for Healing

I will always be grateful to a special client, Judy, and her daughter, Hana, who took my "Stress to Inner Peace" course together. Before that, I hadn't considered working with multiple family members. At the time, Judy was feeling stressed and overwhelmed as she cared for her aging mother. Judy's emotional pain and her mother's increasing care also affected her daughter Hana. As a high-achiever, 15-year-old Hana had been experiencing more pressure at school and at home, so Judy thought Hana could benefit from these tools as well. Since I was already coaching Judy, I thought, "Why not?"

As it turns out, they experienced a beautiful mother-daughter connection through our work together. Judy and Hana became accountability partners and helped one another to remember to practice. In between our sessions, the two would do the meditation tools and techniques together reinforcing their learning and bond. Learning these tools enabled them to involve other family members. After this experience, I understood how powerful a family practice could be. I now encourage families, if possible, to learn these tools together.

Over the past decade, thousands of research studies have found meditation and guided imagery to be effective for reducing the effects of stress-based illnesses, alleviate emotional problems like depression and anxiety and aid in physical healing. Stress and our fearful thoughts can also worsen just about any health condition. Stress seems to increase the risk of obesity, heart disease, immune disorders, Alzheimer's disease, diabetes, depression, gastrointestinal problems, and asthma. Researchers have shown how chronic stress breaks down the body, making it susceptible to disease.[1]

We now have scientific proof that the use of complementary medicine may help relieve stress and repair the body so it can overcome disease. This includes guided imagery and meditation. Some of the other modalities include; Reiki, Healing Touch, therapeutic massage, acupuncture, chiropractic care, herbal medicine, supplements, aromatherapy, and more.

Guided imagery and meditation may also enhance brain function. Neuroscientists, through brain scans, can see how meditation lights up the creative part of our brain, the neocortex, and lowers brain impulses in the amygdala, also known as the "Fight or Flight" part of the brain.

What this means is that you can improve your health and happiness through a regular practice of meditation and guided imagery. This may affect your genes and how they are expressed, called epigenetics, or even your DNA. In Bruce Lipton's book, *Biology of Belief*, he points out how you perceive your reality affects your genes and whether or not you may get a certain disease. Lipton discovered that genes and DNA are constantly evolving and that DNA is controlled by pulsating signals beyond the cells. Positive or negative thoughts also play a huge role in how genes unfold.

Seeing benefits from meditation and guided imagery doesn't take that long either. One Harvard study[2] showed changes in the brain can appear after only eight weeks of mindfulness training, meditation, and guided imagery. The scan results seem to indicate more gray matter has developed. The scan also reports more cognitive functioning and a reduction in the size of the fear areas of the brain. I've witnessed changes in my clients within a few weeks.

Guided imagery has been shown to be helpful to children. A study by the University of Arizona, Tucson, found that chronic stomach pain was reduced by sixty-seven percent in children who participated in guided imagery exercises and practiced relaxation techniques compared to those who did not receive these treatments.[3] In their book, *ADHD in Preschool Children: Assessment and Treatment*, authors Jaswinder Ghuman and Hariwinder Ghuman note that meditation and guided imagery taught to school-age children with ADHD report significant improvements in overall ADHD, inattention, anxiety, and depression.[4]

In my own practice, we tested a guided imagery program that I had created for naptime at early childhood and daycare centers, called *Sleepytime Dreams*. We received anecdotal evidence from six different testing sites. Childcare directors reported the children fell asleep easier and stayed asleep longer and woke up more refreshed. It even calmed children with autism and ADHD, and those living in foster care.

For centuries, spiritual masters believed that if we could still the body, we could calm the mind. As a Certified Guided Imagery Practitioner, I've seen positive results within a few weeks after clients start practicing meditation and using guided imagery. Initially, I ask them to set aside just five minutes and then slowly add minutes as it becomes more ingrained. It's like building a muscle—the more you use these tools, the stronger and more resilient you become. Over time, the benefits of this practice multiply.

Many people have the notion that you must sit on a cushion on the floor in a pretzel position. You might be happy to read that this isn't necessary. What is essential is to be comfortably seated, whatever that means for you. Most of the time, I sit in a chair with my back supported. If you choose to sit on the floor, make sure you have a pillow under your hips.

Once you're comfortable, close your eyes, and focus on your breath. Breathe in through your nose and out through your mouth. How you breathe during this stillness is essential. Breathe in deeply, expanding below the diaphragm into the belly. The breath first fills the lower area and then expands into the upper chest, as though you are filling up a balloon. The Balloon Breath exercise, as well as a breathing technique used by the U.S. Military and Navy SEALs, will be outlined later in this chapter. Both will help you master your breath for calm and focus.

Being More Mindful: Connect to the Breath

We hear so much about mindfulness these days. Author Jon Kabat-Zinn is credited with developing the Mindfulness-Based Stress Reduction (MBSR) program at hospitals to help patients dealing with chronic pain or other physical or mental problems. Now it's used in many settings.

The practice of mindfulness is really the act of being aware of the present moment and accepting this awareness exactly as it is, without judgment, not trying to change it, just noticing and appreciating. The definition from Merriam-Webster's Dictionary[5]:

1: the quality or state of being **mindful**. 2: the practice of maintaining a nonjudgmental state of heightened or complete awareness of one's thoughts, emotions, or experiences on a moment-to-moment basis; also, a state of awareness.

In essence, you are allowing yourself *to be* in a neutral state, focused on the NOW. By being present, you aren't experiencing anxious thoughts in the future or guilt from the past. You are only observing the present moment, without judgment.

Anytime I feel myself in an anxious state and not breathing deeply enough, I know I need to take a mindful breath in and then let it out very slowly. If I do this for one minute just breathing in and out slowly with my eyes opened or closed, it brings me to the present moment. This calms my brain and body and awakens me to the now. And, of course, as I am writing this section, I'm doing this relaxed breathing. I invite you to do the same. Breathe in deeply and then let it out very slowly. As you do this, I invite you to close your eyes for two minutes. You will be amazed at how calm you will feel in that brief time.

Navy SEALs' Box Breath for Calm

Most of my guided imagery scripts and recordings for adults begin with my *16-Seconds to Bliss* because it's one of the fastest ways to calm the body. It turns out, the U.S. Military trains elite Navy SEALs with this same technique, except they call it the *Box Breath* because they maintain focus by picturing a box and breathing around its sides.[6] If these elite warriors who face trauma and the unknown can practice this breathing technique, so can we to help us feel more centered and calm.

As a side note, every time you see Lucy the Llama charater, it's a reminder of a breathing exercise, meditation, or guided imagery script to try. When you see Lucy the Llama with hearts and flowers in her mouth this means the exercise or guided meditation is especially suited for children, ages five and up. Yet, parents and teens are welcome to join in, too.

When you see Lucy Llama with sunglasses that means the exercise or guided meditation is meant for teens, however, parents and adults are also welcome to use them.

When you see Colorful Lucy, this illustration is used to signal helpful exercises for parents, and possibly the whole family to use, or that we have "Cool Tips" to share.

Our first breathing exercise together is *Breathe like a Navy SEAL for Calm and Focus*. Let's first practice this 16-Seconds to Bliss or the Box Breath for two minutes. Later, you may try it for five minutes. The elite SEALs use this before and after important missions to remain calm and sharp.

Breathe Like a Navy SEAL for Calm and Focus

To help relieve stress and tension, we're going to take a few deep breaths in and out in a certain way to bring calm and focus, like how the Navy SEALs are trained. It's known as the Box Breath or 16-seconds to Bliss. For those who have breathing difficulties, you may reduce the count to three or two. Choose what is best for you. For younger children, you may have them practice this same breathing technique. Instead of counting to four, they would breathe in, then hold for a second, breathe out, then hold for a second, and repeat for a minute or so. It's the holding briefly that signals the body to relax. This audio recording is for older children, teens, or adults.

Let's first breathe in and out slowly from our belly. You should feel the belly and ribs on your side expanding, as you breathe in. Now let it out. Good. Put your hand on your belly this time. Try this one more time breathing slowly and deeply, your belly pushing out. Now let the air out. This is how singers are taught to breathe. As you practice, you will get better at this deep breathing.

So now, get comfortable, either sitting up straight in a chair or lying down. Uncross your arms and legs. Now close your eyes, if you will, or find a spot on the wall or floor to focus on while you practice this box breathing. Okay, let's get started. Begin first by blowing out your air… Great. Now, take a breath in deeply on the count of four, 1, 2, 3, 4. Hold for four, 1, 2, 3, 4. Now breathe out on the count of four, 1, 2, 3, 4. Hold once more for four, 1, 2, 3, 4. Breathe in again on the count of four, this time on your own… (Pause for counting) Hold for four…Breathe out on four…. Hold for four…Breathe in again …Hold……Breathe out…. And Hold…Keep breathing and counting for the next minute or so on your own… (Pause for 1-minute more.). Beautiful… You're doing great! Now let's gently open our eyes if they were closed. Notice the sensations in your mind and body. Hopefully, you are feeling calmer, focused, and alert.

You and your child will benefit greatly from learning how to control your breath. As you master breathing in and out slowly, you'll become more grounded in your body. Your thoughts will also calm, moving away from upsetting thoughts into a state of present moment awareness.

You will find audio recordings of this and the next breathing game the *Balloon Breath for Calm* on our website. Make sure to receive your special gift with more opportunities at **InnerPowerMindset.com/IPNgift.**

The *Balloon Breath* is used in several of the guided imagery scripts in subsequent chapters. If your child is hearing-impaired, you can give her instructions so she can practice on her own with eyes closed. After a few minutes, you can tap her on the shoulder to let her know that she can return from the breathing game or guided imagery session. Then let her share what she saw or experienced. The next few breathing exercises are especially geared for children.

The Balloon Breath for Calm (Ages 5 and up.)

Let's imagine that you are blowing up a balloon. What color is it? Then see letting the air out very slowly through the tip of the balloon. Now pretend that your upper body is the balloon. So, as you fill up the balloon, the breath goes deep into your belly, and you then breathe out slowly. So, place your hands on your tummy. That's good. As you breathe in deeply, feel it coming in and out….in and out…as your belly rises and falls. If you place your hands on the side around your ribs area, you will feel that expand as well, as you breathe and expand like a balloon. For children, you can have them lie down and place a stuffed animal on his or her belly and watch it go up and down. That's a fun game, and it puts you in touch with the belly breath.

Let's practice again even slower. We're going to take a deep belly breath in on a count of 3. Breathe in 1, 2, 3. (Pause briefly) Then, slowly breathe out 1, 2, 3. (If this is too much for you or your child, you may change the number and count to 2 each time.) Feel the breath coming in your nose and out slowly from the mouth. Try this again for a few more times and this time close your eyes. Breathe in through your nose and breathe out through your mouth. If it's too hard to breathe in through your nose, you may also breathe in and out through your mouth.

Breathe in 1, 2, 3. Hold it. Then, slowly breath out 1, 2, 3. That's great. Now go ahead and try it on your own for a little bit and I will be quiet for a few moments. (Pause 30 seconds) Beautiful! Now let's come back into the room. Take 2 deep breaths. Wriggle your hands and toes, if possible. Now slowly open your eyes.

A few rounds of this deep breathing can bring a little peace. Counselors and therapists often teach deep breathing technique to their patients who suffer from anxiety and stress. Slow deep breathing stimulates the parasympathetic nervous system, which is responsible for relaxing and slowing down the body and its internal functions. If you're having a stressful day, or gripped by fear or worry, breathing deeply with or without eyes closed can be stress relieving. You will feel more grounded and centered in just a minute or two.

Blowing Out Birthday Candles is another breathing game that can be a soothing and quick way for children to settle down. It's a beautiful way to blow away your troubles. Practice these techniques with your child before he or she is upset. Then, you suggest he practice these mindful games when he's frustrated or scared or just needs to calm down. By breathing in deeply and slowly, we are signaling the body and mind for peace.

The Power of Thoughts

Blowing out Birthday Candles
(Ages 5 and up.)

Blowing out Birthday Candles can help children relax especially when they're having a hard day. And, who doesn't like birthdays? It's a fun game, so be playful.

Now imagine that your fingers are the top of a birthday cake. You will be blowing out each candle....one at a time... very slowly. Each time you blow one candle out, you are blowing away all stress, pain, discomfort, or anger. Whatever is bothering you, blow it all out! As you breathe in again, envision that you are filling yourself with peace.

Take one hand and hold it up, facing you. Spread your fingers wide apart. Good. Let's start with your thumb as a birthday candle. Take a breath in, now imagine you're blowing out the candle on your thumb, letting all of your air out. With that, you're blowing out all discomfort and stress. Then, you're filling back up with peace. (Pause briefly) That's great! Next, go to your pointer or index finger. Imagine that finger lit up with a birthday candle. Take a deep breath and quietly blow out the next candle...blowing out all fear and anger or sadness. (Pause briefly) That's right...so beautiful. On to the third finger, your middle finger, take a big breath and blow out that candle. Let it all go. (Pause briefly) Make sure to fill back up with peace and calm. That's great. Let's move to another candle to blow out what's called the ring finger. See it all lit up? Take one more deep breath. Now blow out that candle. Goodbye stress and pain. And now we move to your pinky finger... number 5. Take a big breath and blow out that candle. You did great!

Now you can breathe normally again...in and out. If needed, you can continue doing the same thing with your other hand, blowing out one candle at a time on each finger. When you're finished, sit quietly, breathing in and out normally. Feel yourself surrounded by more peace and love. When you are ready, shake out your hands and notice how much calmer and softer you feel.

These mindfulness techniques are not new. As mentioned, many psychologists and counselors have been teaching these tools for years. What's new is the acknowledgment that we may all benefit from mindful breathing. These techniques are useful not only for clinical anxiety or panic but are just as effective for everyday experiences. Try them and notice what happens. There are additional mindful techniques and mind-body tools for parents to practice and then share with your children and teens in Chapter 11.

Take a few breaks throughout your day to check in and breathe slowly. This gives your mind a rest and brings your awareness back to your body to just *be* in the present moment. Ahhh...just to breathe and go inside! That is where your true power lies.

CHAPTER 2

The Power of Thoughts

Scientists say we have over sixty-thousand thoughts or more a day. How many of these are empowering? How many are full of worry, doubt, and fear? The Cleveland Clinic reports almost ninety-five percent are negative. Often, eighty percent are the same disempowering thoughts repeat every day.[7] For many of us, fearful thoughts can run amok and lead to anxiety. Psychologists have developed an acronym—F.E.A.R.—to describe this behavior. F.E.A.R. stands for **F**alse **E**vidence **A**ppearing **R**eal. In other words, our minds invent problems that never materialize but feel very real. It's apparently part of human nature, as noted by French philosopher and essayist, Michel de Montaigne, "My life has been filled with terrible misfortune; most of which never happened." He said that in the *sixteenth century*.

An estimated forty million adult Americans suffer from Generalized Anxiety Disorder (GAD) according to the National Institute of Health. Seven million of those suffer from anxiety as a chronic condition. It's also estimated that twenty percent of teens and children suffer from anxiety at some point before adulthood. To make matters worse, children of anxious parents are more at risk to develop an anxiety disorder.[8] It's for our children's future mental health that we present our best selves today. Tuning into calming behaviors, such as meditation and guided imagery, with our children give us the opportunity to be great examples for our children.

One aspect of stress is racing, fearful thoughts that will <u>not</u> stop. Some call this a "monkey mind" as it jumps from one thought to another endlessly. Meditation helps by quieting the overactive mind. Through a regular practice of meditation, being still in body and mind, you will begin to separate your *being* from your thoughts. You become an observer of those thoughts, but you don't become or stay entangled in them.

During meditation, you become more aware of the present moment and part of All-That-Is from a detached and centered place. When a thought or external trigger pulls you out of your center, you can dispassionately observe, "Oh, that's just another fearful thought," and then refocus on your breath and your inner stillness. Simply noticing the thought will help it melt away. A thought really is just a thought, and you can let it pass through you. At the same time, you may begin to start questioning your thoughts as being helpful or not. "Is this thought coming from my wiser self or from my anxiety, or my ego-driven lower self?"

You may be wondering how our thoughts affect us. In 1994, Dr. Masaru Emoto began photographing water crystals. The experiment began by using water from various sources: tap water, polluted rivers and lakes, and pristine rivers and lakes. Their initial photographs were taken with a high-powered microscope and a special camera. The images were telling. Tap water and polluted water produced distorted, ugly crystals. Water from pristine sources produced beautiful crystals.

They then took the experiment further, wanting to know if the beauty of the water crystal could be influenced. This time, they used twice-filtered water produced for hospital use to control the water source. Then, each glass of water was shown letters or pictures, had a prayer or word said to it or had music directed at it. The water was then frozen. What they discovered is amazing. The water crystals infused with prayerful thoughts like "Love and Gratitude" or joy formed beautiful patterns. Those with negative thoughts like "You Disgust Me" or anger created patterns that were rough, opaque and in a state of chaos.[9] .

Love and Gratitude
© Office Masaru Emoto, LLC

You Disgust Me
© Office Masaru Emoto, LLC

Consider this: since we're made up of seventy-five percent water, how do you think your thoughts are influencing your body? By harnessing the power of guided imagery and meditation, you can break the cycle of harmful thoughts.

Neuroscientists have discovered that the mind doesn't know the difference between what is real and what is imagined. That's why when you see food, you start to salivate, or if you see a beach image, you can imagine feeling the sun on your face. The mind creates the images, and our senses fill in the rest: how it looks, smells, tastes, or is heard. The body thinks these images are real. The same principle applies to guided imagery. The more full and rich the imagery, the more you will benefit. Seeing images, however, isn't the only way to experience guided imagery.

Sometimes, people may *feel* more than see each suggestion in the meditations. Others may experience sensations related to their other senses, such as smell or taste. These responses are normal. My guided imagery coach and mentor, Sandy Jost is a person who experiences guided imagery through feeling. While she doesn't see vivid images, she still practices and believes in the healing properties of guided imagery. How you experience guided imagery is unique to you. Don't worry about how well you are imagining—just trust your own process and stick with it.

As you go deeper into your guided imagery, you enter an altered brainwave state. A short primer on brainwaves will be helpful to understand why guided imagery and meditation can affect us so profoundly. When we're awake and engaged in a task or conversation, our brain emits beta waves. Our brains are active and processing at high speed. When we enter a guided imagery session or meditation, our brains slow down, emitting alpha waves. In this state, our brains are in a non-aroused state but still engaged. As we move deeper into guided imagery or meditation, our brains slow demonstrably. This is theta. Theta is the state in which great ideas are born. It's also often experienced during repetitive tasks that don't require us to fully pay attention, such as showering or driving on a familiar highway. The final state is Delta, but that's when you're asleep.[10]

Meditation reaches into our subconscious where major healing, growth, learning, and performance improvement can occur. Once we learn how to turn off our "beta brain," we're able to access the more creative and intuitive mind available in alpha and theta. Here, we're less resistant to change and more capable of hearing suggestions that flow to us. It shifts our physiology and biochemistry.

Researchers also point out that meditation builds the "feeling of being in control." Psychology research shows that when we feel a sense of mastery over our lives, we perform better. Guided meditation puts us in a state where we can grow, heal, and transform. A helpful side effect may be that our self-esteem increases, and we develop a true optimism about the future.[11]

Letting Go of Stressful Thoughts

"There is no stress in the world, only people thinking stressful thoughts." When I had first heard this quote from Wayne Dyer, listening to an audiobook *Being in Balance*, I thought, "Wayne, that's easy for you to say, you don't know my crazy, stress-filled world and all the stuff that I *have* to get done. But then, I took some time to consider what he actually meant, after his next statement. "No one can create negativity and stress within you, only *you* can do that."[12]

We sometimes cannot control events, but we can control our response to events. Sometimes it's impossible not to think upsetting thoughts, but we have a choice as to how long these thoughts consume us. Life can be disappointing and throw us many curves, such as when facing cancer, or job loss, or other misfortunes. It's perfectly normal to think angry or fearful thoughts. Yet, we also have control over our response to the event and our attitude toward it.

What is your everyday worldview (putting aside what your child is currently going through)? Is that the world is wonderful and there are adventures to be had? Or is it more along like life never gives you a break? I know for me, whenever that kind of thinking comes up, I'll end up doing some mindless escape or use my belief as an excuse to run away from feelings and binge on sweets to feel better. How we view life matters, not only to us but to those around us. The hard truth is that we have a choice in each moment whether to succumb to critical thoughts or challenge that all-or-nothing thinking. Here's what you could do when you find yourself churning a bad thought. You could change course slightly to grab a better thought. You could also take a mindful breath to bring you to the present moment. Or you might want to move your body by taking a walk or getting some exercise to release the negative energy. The bottom line is that you don't have to stay stuck!

Quick Practices to Help with Stress

We know as a busy mom or dad, you have a lot to do and many responsibilities. Here are some briefer ways to add more calm. Below are two examples of brief meditations to help you let go of the noise. *Breathing Space for Calm* is a great practice to check in and get centered by taking a few slow deep breaths for two or three minutes. You can do this at any time to relieve stress. I even put a mindfulness bell on my smartphone. Set the soft bell or soft chimes to ring a few times a day to remind yourself to take a break in your day to be present.

You don't have to sit pretzel-style in a lotus position to meditate. You may sit comfortably in a chair. It's helpful to sit

The Power of Thoughts

up straight and not too rigid. You may also sit on a meditation cushion or bench. When you do the breathing, breathe in through your nose and then breath out through your mouth. Let's practice an exercise called *Breathing Space for Calm.* You'll notice colorful Lucy Llama for families and Teen Lucy.

As a note for the various meditation practices and guided imagery, I recommend that you try them with and without soft calming music or adding ambient sounds, like ocean waves or gentle rain. Adding music and sound may add to a more relaxing experience and can help block the outside noises, so you are more focused on the inside.

Breathing Space for Calm

This is Breathing Space for Calm. Begin by sitting up straight, yet relaxed. Uncross your arms and legs. Now tune into calm and go inside with the intention of waking up to a presence of greater awareness.

Step 1. *Focus on what is happening right now. Accept your present moment, without trying to change anything... dropping into stillness and awareness. Tuning into whatever is here at the moment. Whatever it is occurring is all okay... Notice any thoughts ...what's in your mind...notice emotions, as well...then become aware of any body sensations...opening* up to all of it ...just as it is. Explore in a gentle way without having to change anything.

Step 2. *Becoming more aware of your breath. Let it just be as you feel all sensations related to breathing in and out...not changing it ...but allowing each breath to breathe itself. And closely tuning into each in breath and each out breath...moment by moment.*

Step 3. *Expand your awareness even further. Notice sensations throughout the body...feeling the whole body ... and if you notice areas of intense sensation...let them be. Holding them with compassion and acceptance...as you do this, you'll be more open to experiencing whatever occurs throughout the rest of your day. You are welcome to return and tune into this breathing space meditation at any time ... to refresh your mind and body.*

Inner Peace Time is another way to take a break from all the noise and go inside. In this brief meditation, you will use a phrase to help you let go and unwind. Throughout centuries, spiritual leaders have used mantras, prayers or words, to keep the conscious mind occupied in order to reach a deeper mind for calm and inspiration. One hint that I'd like to pass along. In meditation, you will continue to notice thoughts. They will come and go, as well as their associated feelings. What you'll want to do is not attach to the thought. You may notice, "Oh there's another thought." Then, let it go to float away like clouds. Return back to your breath or mantra.

Inner Peace Time for Parents, Teens, and Older Children

To begin the "Inner Peace" meditation, get into a comfortable position. Close your eyes or find a spot on the floor or wall to focus on, if closing your eyes is uncomfortable. Then tune in to your breathing by slowly breathing in and out. As you breathe in, think "peace." As you do this, feel a beautiful white healing light of love or a rainbow of colors filling up your entire body. That's great. As you breathe out, think, "free" or "release." Now let go of any stress or worry thoughts.

Closing your eyes connects you with your imagination. Breathe in again and as you say "peace," feel the love coming into your body. Breathe out "release," feel yourself let go, and allow it to expand out from your body. Keep doing this for a few minutes or as long as you like. Just a few minutes can make a big difference tuning into calm. If any thoughts, noises, or discomfort is experienced, just return to the phrase. It's like a mantra, a phrase to keep your thinking brain busy, so you may reach the deeper part of your mind and inner power.

Keeping breathing in peace and letting go for a few more minutes. As you do, feel yourself waking up to a loving presence.

Inner Peace Time is a simple way to begin meditating. Try this for a couple of minutes, and then build up to five minutes. Add another five minutes each week with the goal of meditating for 20 minutes. Even if you've tried meditating before, begin fresh. It's helpful to let go of any past resistance. It's always best to start each time you meditate with a beginner's mind. Be open with a feeling of waking up…waking up to a larger awareness of peace, love, and healing.

Heart and Brain Coherence

Researchers have discovered that the brain and heart are constantly in communication. There are neurotransmitters in the heart and brain that send messages back and forth. When we feel angry, anxious, or overwhelmed, our brain and heart are out-of-sync and not in coherence, which adds to our stress. When they are in coherence and beat in harmony, we feel calmer.

According to HeartMath Institute's Science of the Heart, the heart's electro-magnetic field measures 40 to 60 times greater than the human brain. Scientists now back up what spiritual leaders have known for centuries—the enormous power of the heart. [13]

There are ways to bring the heart and brain quickly into harmony and coherence. If we can bring the heart and mind together in rhythm through loving thoughts, we will feel more peaceful. When we are in stress-mode, they are not in coherence. You'll be surprised how quickly we bring coherence. The parents that I coach at a pediatric hospital enjoy this fast way to connect to their hearts and let go of stress.

Quick Heart Coherence (Freeze Technique)

One way to bring yourself back into balance and into coherence more quickly is to practice this Heart Coherence "Freeze Technique." This is a great stress reliever with benefits lasting for several hours. This exercise developed by the HeartMath Institute may be performed by all ages, including children four-years-old and up.

Step 1: Begin by putting your hand over your heart, or a finger on your chest area to connect to your heart space within. Then, begin slow deep breathing in and out. This sends messages to the brain and nervous system that you are beginning to feel safe. Next, close your eyes and start slowly breathing in and out of your heart. If this feels awkward then imagine calmly breathing in and out of your chest.

Step 2: Then, add <u>one</u> of these positive feelings: compassion, gratitude, caring, love or appreciation. Adding one positive elevated emotion helps raise the power of love and seems to magnetize a warm feeling in your heart and brain.

Step 3: Now add an image in your mind of someone or something that you really love and brings a lot of joy of unconditional love. Your feelings of calm and safety will be magnetized even more. Stay here in quick coherence for at least two minutes. You may even feel your heart expanding and opening up to a greater awareness of love. That's great. This exercise can be healing to you and those you love as you keep expanding your heart. You may also continue in this heart coherence for as long as you like.

It's advised to do this for two-minutes and soon you will feel more peaceful. The HeartMath Institute researchers, who studied this technique, claim this coherence will last for several hours or more in your mind and body. Practice this a few times a day to become more familiar with the exercise and expand your heart with positive feelings for heart coherence healing. At an advanced meditation workshop, I witnessed hundreds of people doing this together and honestly, I had never felt my heart feel so expansive, so full of love and compassion.

An Attitude of Gratitude

Gratitude is the single most important ingredient to living a successful and fulfilled life.
--Jack Canfield

Having an attitude of gratitude is one of the healthier things we may do with our thoughts. Much scientific research is focusing on the power of gratitude to boost happiness. Dr. Robert Emmons, author of *Thanks: How the New Science of Gratitude Can Make You Happier,* cites recent studies on how a gratitude practice affects the mind and body: [14]

- A gratitude practice reduces perceived stress by 28% and depression by 16%
- Gratitude is related to 23% lower levels of the stress hormone cortisol
- Writing a letter of gratitude reduced feelings of hopelessness by 88% of suicidal inpatients and increased levels of optimism in 94% of them
- Gratitude is related to a 10% improvement in sleep quality in patients with chronic pain.

The Power of Thoughts

Simply believing you are grateful for blessings does not bring more happiness. You need to put it into practice. Try this exercise "Find 3 Good Things," for two weeks in a row. Take out a sheet of paper and write down three good things each day and do it with your children. This will help you focus on the positive, happier moments and things to appreciate and may help lift your mood. Others have kept a gratitude journal and these are quite helpful to help you focus on the good in your life. You can also do the Quick Heart Coherence exercise—this time focusing on the three things for which you are grateful.

CHAPTER 3

Unleash Your Imagination

I can still remember the first time I participated in a group guided meditation. In the imagery, we went on a magical journey to create a safe sanctuary. Decades later, I can still recall this illuminated place of love and healing. I see a glittering glass ceiling that opens to allow a shimmering golden light to descend, bathing me in total peace. That first time, it felt like I was watching a movie in my mind. That's what imagery does. It creates a movie in your mind complete with sounds, pictures, and feelings.

The practice of guided imagery is based on the idea that your body responds as though what you are imagining is real. Using all your senses, you see and feel a detailed scene in your mind of what you would most like to experience in your life. What do you see? What do you feel? What do you hear? What does it smell like? The more you practice using all your senses in this relaxed state, the deeper you will go, where real change can take place. In some ways, it's like hypnosis, where you reach a very relaxed, subconscious state receptive to positive suggestions, thoughts, and feelings.

The main difference between guided imagery and hypnosis is that instead of listening to an external voice giving suggestions, as in hypnosis, guided imagery gives you access to your loving inner wisdom and an opening to an energy source or God to help in the healing process. When you add an emotional charge (empowering feelings) around this multisensory visualization, you send a powerful intention to your inner power to reach your goals.

There is power in your perception. How you perceive your reality affects your reality. Dr. Joe Dispenza in his research with his advanced meditation workshop participants showed real changes in scanned images of the brain as well as these meditators feeling changes in their health. With guided imagery and meditation, you may enter a pure state of consciousness to a feeling of coherence in which you become more of a creator rather than a reactor to life. Being in a state of elevated emotion and gratitude aids this process.

Over the past few decades, the effectiveness of guided imagery has been increasingly proven by research that shows its positive impact on health, creativity, and performance. In a study of diabetic patients, even ten to fifteen minutes of imagery can reduce blood pressure and lower cholesterol and glucose levels in the blood. It also heightens the immune function in the cells.

According to the website, *Health Journey*, guided imagery can reduce blood loss during surgery and the need for morphine afterward. It lessens headaches and pain. It can increase a person's skill at skiing, tennis, writing, and singing. It accelerates weight loss and reduces anxiety. It has reduced the adverse effects of chemotherapy and radiation therapy, especially nausea, depression, soreness, and fatigue.[15]

Guided imagery taps into the right hemisphere, the creative side of the brain. Because all we need is our imagination, a great benefit of creative visualization is that you can do it with a guided imagery practitioner or on your own when it's convenient for you.

Doing meditation or guided imagery is a great way to start or end your day. Even if you only practice for five or ten minutes in the morning, by focusing on gratitude and peace, you set the tone for your day. You may also end your day with a few minutes of reflection and appreciation, even if it's simply noticing those little things we often overlook. By noticing and focusing on the good things in our lives, those things will expand. Be open to your desires and true intentions to what matters most.

As mentioned earlier in meditation or guided imagery, you will continue to notice thoughts. They will come and go, as will their associated feelings. Best thing is not to attach to the thought. You may notice your to-do list, for example. Just let that thought dissolve or float away like clouds. Then return to your breathing or sounds, if you're listening to guided imagery. Consider recording this guided meditation so you can relax fully while doing it. Just make sure to read it slowly and pause in between phrases to get the full relaxation effect to reach your deeper mind.

The most important thing is that you feel safe to experiment with new ideas, dreams, and desires. If my words and guided meditations can help you open just a little bit more to healing, peace, and happiness, then this is my gift to you. Before beginning this morning meditation, come to a place of gratitude. Then set an intention of how you want to create your day. Please note: if you've experienced hallucinations, or if you or your child have been diagnosed with schizophrenia, it is advised <u>not</u> to practice guided imagery. You may still meditate. Always feel free to discuss with your doctor.

Morning Light Meditation

As you begin your day, make sure you are in a quiet space where you will not be disturbed. Relax and get into a comfortable position. Sit up straight, uncross your arms and legs, and place your hands in your lap. If you are lying down, place your arms by your sides. Now take 4 deep breaths in and out. Breathe in on a count of 4…1, 2, 3, 4, then hold for 4…1, 2, 3, 4 and release on a count of 4. (Pause briefly) If this is too difficult, you may breathe in on a count of 3 or 2. But make sure to pause. This will calm you, so take your time to breathe in slowly a few more times and just let go. (Pause 20 seconds)

See a beautiful white light come in from above. Let this beautiful, loving light pour into the top of your head into your forehead, temples, eyes, and mouth, letting go of tension. As the beautiful light travels through your body, feel your shoulders totally let go with this beautiful white light. Your arms and hands relax, too. Feel your back unwind, into your core and center of your being. Notice any remaining tension and let it all go in…your hips, legs, and feet. Stay in this peaceful bliss for a few moments. (Pause 10 seconds)

As your body feels this serenity, feel the light of wisdom and inspiration pour out from your heart as you connect with your inner coach. (Pause 10 seconds) Feel grounded in loving support from Mother Earth as well. (Pause briefly) Feel this illumination as a column of light surrounding you. Your heart expands and connects to your inner wisdom surrounded by a beautiful white light from above and below. (Pause briefly)

Now begin to think about the day you're about to create and visualize this day, coming from your heart. How would you like it to be? See every event unfolding just as you would like it ideally. Pretend you see before you a circle of light. You can put anything that you want to occur in the glow of energy that surrounds you. If you want better health, put that in, more abundance and love, add those, too. See your relationships all going well. What about your relationships to money and success? Imagine abundance flowing to you. How about a little love and joy? Add those to your energy field. Add other blessings that you truly desire. (Pause 20 seconds)

Everything is happening beautifully. If you're having trouble visualizing, then just feel or sense how great your day will unfold. It's your blessing of light. And you may choose the qualities you most want, so keep adding. (Pause 20 seconds)

Now say to yourself but not out loud:

- *I bless my day with love and light. (Pause briefly)*
- *I bless myself with pure loving energy. (Pause briefly)*

Repeat this one more time to yourself.

- *I bless my day with love and light. (Pause briefly)*
- *I bless myself with pure source energy. (Pause briefly)*

You may bless others, too. (Pause 20 seconds). Carry this joy for yourself and others throughout your day. For today, the present is a gift, a beautiful gift. And you are grateful.

Now it's time to bring your awareness back into this room, gently back to the space you're in. You feel energized from all that you have received. And now, you sense where you are sitting or lying. You feel fully refreshed and alert. And when you're ready, open your eyes. Welcome back.

What's great about this *Morning Light* guided meditation is that you can do one for each child. Put in what you most want for each child to experience in his or her day like healing, better health, making friends, doing well in school, and feeling loved, or whatever else you desire. You can also teach this morning meditation to your children when they're older or as teens.

Guided imagery is a tool for focusing your imagination on behaviors or events that you want to occur positively in your life. These are imagined at a deeper level of your mind that bypasses your conscious state, to that place that connects to your inner power. Whether you're seeking better health and healing, more prosperity, better relationships, or for more peace and calm; guided imagery can help you achieve it.

Psychologist and best-selling author Gay Hendricks believes that visualization or guided imagery is one of the most powerful tools for change. Many people are stuck by events of the past, but visualization is creating your future self in the present. Hendricks says, "Visualization changes the dynamics of personal change by pulling the person toward a visualized healthier future."[16]. It's like a magnet attracting that vision into reality.

There's even greater impact by repeating the same visualization for three to four weeks straight. Scientists believe there's something in the brain that rewires in this timeframe called the Reticular Activating System. In a study done by NASA, astronauts had to wear a set of glasses that turned their world upside down for thirty days.[17]

The astronauts were told to wear the glasses twenty-four hours a day, seven days a week. What they learned from the study surprised the researchers. The astronauts who wore the glasses as instructed discovered that between twenty-one and thirty days, their brains re-interpreted their worldview to right side up. Researchers also found that if the glasses were removed before the twenty-one to thirty-day interval, the astronaut would have to start over. This experiment shows how powerful our brain is at rewiring itself.

Interestingly, guided imagery and meditation rewire the brain, too. To have the most lasting changes and be most effective, it's advised to practice guided imagery or meditation for at least twenty-one to thirty days in a row.

Journaling

It's also a good idea to have a journal handy to capture images, feelings or words that may appear during guided imagery. Have paper available for your child, as well. Tell your loved one to write from his heart any special feelings or messages that are received. You or your child may want to draw a picture that you received during the meditation. Words may also pop into your head or answer a question you have had. It's also a great way to express feelings.

Most important is to remain open to what may come and enjoy the ride. With imagery, you will explore a wonderful, healing journey. Because of your relaxed state, you connect with your deeper and subconscious minds. Tapping into these brain-states allows you to be open to change or to view situations in a new light.

Always know that you are in charge and no one can make you do anything you don't want to do or see something you don't want to see. Anytime you or your child feel unsafe, you can travel to your safe space where you'll be wrapped in a blanket of peace, safety, love, and appreciation. The next chapter has a guided imagery called *Discovering Your Safe Place*, which is geared toward children. However, teens and adults also will benefit from discovering a safe sanctuary.

Soul-Soothing Guided Meditations

Many guided imagery meditations for children are featured in the upcoming chapters. While these are written for children, I invite you to do them together. As the parent or caregiver, I want you to be a part of this journey. Please remember doing guided imagery and mindful tools can be quite powerful and fun. Teens are also welcome to use them as well.

As you do these guided imagery sessions, please be open to the healing adventures that will benefit you both. You and your child will journey into discovering a safe place, opening your heart to loving kindness, meeting your inner guide, creating freedom from fear, healing your body, finding pain relief, and promoting restorative sleep. The book ends with a few chapters for teens and adults that includes guided imagery for a more mature audience.

Children ten and older can read the chapters alone, or you may read together. It's best as a shared experience. I also recommend that you read the guided imagery scripts out loud to your child, while he or she experiences the mental imagery. We've included a friendly character Lucy the Llama to help make your child feel loved and safe.

Part 2

For Children and Teens

CHAPTER 4

Your Safe Place to Heal for Children and Teens

Special Message for Kids!

Lucy the Llama

You are very special and a superhero. Lucy the Llama and I don't know what you may be facing. All we know is how brave you, your parents, and other caregivers are. We're here to offer you a little calm and comfort in your day. We also know that you have a wiser part that lies within your heart. If you don't know where that is, please ask your mom or dad to find your heart center, which I call your "Heart Star."

We all have this amazing inner light that is more powerful than we can imagine. It's like our inner wizard that connects us to the powerful love of the Universe, or some call this God, or Source, or the Divine. You come from love and are so very loved. Lucy the Llama is also here to remind us of our inner guide. Llamas are special because if you see one, it reminds us to *keep an open heart, stay positive, give thanks, and follow guidance to live your dreams.*

Please know this. You are NOT to blame for any illness, disease, or health problem. For some reason, you're facing this experience together with your family—the good and bad times. I have created these imagery stories and meditations to help you have less pain and suffering and to bring in a power of healing and comfort that is available at any time. Remember this: YOU are the powerful one. You will be doing the healing. I am just a connector and reminder of your shining star.

Even though we haven't met, I love you and want you to know that you are a miracle. You are my superhero! Lucy the Llama loves you, too. We are stronger together than alone. Lucy and I are amazed by you!

Please remember, anytime you see Lucy Llama with flowers in her mouth, that means it's a meditation especially for kids. As a side note, these guided meditations are appropriate for ages 6 and up—so that means they're worthy for teens and parents, too!

Your Safe Place to Heal for Children and Teens

Special Message for Teens!

It's so challenging being a teen these days. You have so many demands! Schoolwork, sports, or music lessons and activities, to name a few. It can be very stressful. When faced with a serious illness, the pressure may feel overwhelming and not fair. I totally agree. Your illness or health challenge is not fair, and you aren't to blame for any of this. You may be feeling different than others, or more separated from friends. Your appearance may be changing, and you may also fear the unknown.

You face enormous challenges as a teen or young adult. These changes in your life and health are tough, but what I do know is that within you, there's an amazing inner coach who can help with feeling more love, peace, and less stress. This superpower can be enhanced with tools like meditation and guided imagery.

New research published by the American Psychological Association shows teens may experience higher levels of stress than adults (during the school year.) [18] Yet, teens don't have great ways to relieve stress. Most popular are video games or surfing the internet. While these may be stress reducing, they may not be building resilience to help teens cope better with difficulties in life.

This is where meditation, guided imagery, and mindfulness can help. Research shows that when teens practice meditation and guided imagery, it can lower rates of anxiety and depression, and may help with sleep. It can also help with schoolwork and focus, as well as build stronger relationships.

Think of the thoughts in your mind like monkeys flying from one tree to the next. Once you slow down this "monkey mind" and tune into your heart, you will engage a deeper mind and loving presence that can aid stress relief and healing, and so much more. Please feel free to use any of the guided imagery stories and games that follow. They're appropriate for all ages. I also include a special chapter just for you. Chapter 9, Inner Power for Teens, contains several guided imagery lessons, including *Empowering Self-Esteem*, and *Loving Coach Inner Guide.*

Be open, unleash your imagination, and trying something new. Let's call upon your body's innate healing and a loving presence for healing and an empowered life. For teens, anytime you see this image of Lucy Llama with sunglasses, this is a meditation geared especially for you.

Please note that Chapters 4 through 8 have many healing and empowering guided meditations for your health and happiness. Chapter 9 has several guided imagery examples just for teens! All are welcome to enjoy the journey throughout the next four chapters, including our first guided imagery in this chapter about discovering your safe place. As a reminder please note: if your child or teen has been diagnosed with schizophrenia or experienced delusions, it is advised not to practice guided imagery. Your child may still meditate. Always feel free to discuss with your child's doctor.

Journey Through Your Imagination: Finding Your Safe Place

Are you ready for some fun? With guided imagery, it's like make-believe with SUPERPOWERS, like being a superhero. You use your imagination to create magical places and adventures. You already use your imagination during playtime, or when you daydream in class. It's like playing a movie in your mind. That's what imagery is all about. The difference will be that what we create during *Inner Power NOW* will be positive and healing so you will feel less stress and pain.

Enjoy using all your senses, like what you see, hear, touch, and smell during imagery. You may also feel joy, love, being thankful, or a sense of peace. When you combine all of this together, you will journey on a grand adventure to an enchanted place of love and healing to help you feel better. Be open to whatever you see, hear, or feel.

Sometimes children or teens think they're not doing guided imagery in the right way because they don't see images. Whatever you feel, see, hear, or imagine will be just right for you. Some kids see better, while others hear better. Then, there are those children that just sense a place or a feeling. All senses are welcome.

One of the best tools to use in imagery is your ability to discover and create a safe, loving place—that's just for *you*. Your parents and caregivers can also do this, so they find a safe space, too. This can be any place that you want it to be. Having a safe place to go, means you can be yourself there. It can be in a beautiful setting outdoors, indoors, or a dreamy fairytale.

One child may create a colorful, cozy cave. Another might imagine a safe space with a magical carpet that takes her to faraway places. Parents may want to escape to a more relaxed and sacred place. They might imagine escaping to a beach or beautiful golden temple or lush garden, just to relax and feel renewed. Once you create your special place, it feels so real that you might have a change in attitude as you escape the pressures of life. What's more, you can return to it at any time to help you feel safe and at peace.

Some teens or adults might be a little self-conscious when trying guided imagery for the first time or two. This is normal. But often once they try it, the experience is so powerful that they find they enjoy the process. They just need to allow themselves to go into fantasy and be okay with whatever appears or does not appear.

Many children have found retreating to their safe space helps new medicals tests be less painful. Before the test, they go to their imaginary safe space, where they feel happy, loved, and protected. You can try this, too! You can even take Lucy Llama with you to help you be not so afraid. Whatever place you create will be just right for you.

Parents or caregivers, you can either read this slowly to your child, pausing to make sure you give time for the movie in your child's mind to unfold. Or, you can listen to the recording together at our website. It's always good to start with some deep breathing and relaxation. Make sure to pause in between phrases for best results. As a reminder, you may add soft, calming music for a more relaxing and healing experience.

Discover Your Safe Place

Let's begin with the Balloon Breath. Now settle into a comfortable position either sitting in a chair or lying down, with your hands in your lap or by your sides. If you want, you can close your eyes. That's great. Feel as though you are breathing and filling up a balloon. Breathe in on a count of three slowly…1…2…3, then breathe out again on a count of three 1…2…3… (keep breathing like this for a few moments). (Pause for 20 seconds)

Now, imagine a beautiful white light all around you. (Pause briefly) This glowing healing light is now erasing any stress, pain, or tension in your body. Feel this beautiful light that helps you let go from your head to your toes… Notice any remaining tension or stress in your body, and tell it to relax, more and more deeply… Feeling so very relaxed. (Pause briefly)

Let's imagine you are walking down 3 steps, and as you go down each step, you are becoming more calm and relaxed. By the time you reach the bottom step, you are very relaxed. So, let's count from 3 down to 2. Now down to 1…. You are so very calm and at peace. (Pause briefly) Imagine a lovely path that you are now walking along. As it winds around… what do you see? What sounds? Or smells? Take it all in as you keep walking… This path is taking you to your special place.

Up ahead you see a magic carpet that is waiting just for you. This magic carpet will carry you to your special place… As you sit down on the magic carpet, it gently lifts you up. Enjoy the ride as it safely carries you along your journey. (Pause briefly) Up ahead, you see a magical place that's waiting for you. The magic carpet gently lands. You are happy to easily slide off the magic carpet. You see up ahead a colorful, amazing door, and you know behind that door is your place to feel safe and loved. You walk up and turn the golden knob and open the door. (Pause briefly)

What do you see? (Pause briefly) This place can be any place that is calm, relaxing and feels very good to you. (Pause briefly) Are you outside or inside? It can be on an island, by the ocean, a forest, the inside of a castle, or any place you choose. You walk around and take in the beauty. Here is your special place of love and healing. You feel good about yourself in your safe spot, and here you are surrounded by all the things that make you happy. (Pause briefly)

You can play or rest or invite your favorite people to join you. Whenever someone comes in, you feel accepted and loved just the way you are.... You are so special. Spend a few moments in your happy, safe place. (Pause 20 seconds) Keep this place in your mind that you will return to again, whenever you need to relax and chill out. Stay here for a few moments, taking in all the sights, sounds, smells. (Pause briefly) Now it's time to leave this special place, but before you go, take it all in once more. You may return anytime you wish. This is your safe place to feel loved and at peace.

So now, coming back into the room where you began... sitting or lying down ... You feel happy and so very loved. If you are listening to this at bedtime...breathe deeply and allow yourself to gently fall asleep... safe until morning or when you need to get up. And if this is your time to wake up, gently bring yourself back, aware of the room you are in and sense where your body is. If you want, you may wiggle your fingers and toes. Now open your eyes.

You may use this script as a starting place. Make sure that you create a place of peace, love, and healing, where you feel totally accepted. All safe places are unique; that's what makes them so special. If you want to choose a different safe place, that's fine, too. You may change it. Whatever feels best.

After you have discovered your safe place, guided imagery, or the movies in your mind, can be launched in all kinds of directions. Often, we may journey to our safe space for relieving stress and worry. We may also meet a special guide, wizard, or animal friend that might have fun gifts for us or great insights or messages. You will go through some of these adventures in the next chapter.

Cool Tips to Know

Remember in your special place, you can try on new skills, fun activities, or behaviors. It's your place of wonder to grow and expand and you can imagine whatever you want to do. Sometimes I'm asked, "What if I don't see pictures in my mind, or I don't see any special place?" That's okay. Sometimes, you may be thinking too hard, and that blocks the images. Maybe you need to let go and relax a little more. Please know that some of us might hear things better, or we might feel something stronger than others. Sometimes, you might sense a special place, but you don't see anything. Whatever you imagine is perfect at that moment. Your imagination is like a muscle. The more you use it, the better you will become at this.

You might also try this. Play a game with your mom or dad and have one of them come up with a story. As they tell the story, close your eyes, and see what comes up. Are you able to imagine the story in your mind? If so, maybe you were just a little afraid or tried too hard the first time we did the *Discover Your Safe Place* imagery. So, let's just try again at a later date. Lucy Llama wants you to know that "All is well and will be well."

CHAPTER 5

Meeting Your Inner Guide or Magical Wizard

I hope you had fun discovering your safe and loving place. Now it's time to expand on that. Once you travel to your safe space, you can bring in a wise inner guide, like a special angel, spiritual guide, or even a magical wizard. You can invite this guide to visit with you in your safe place to help with problems or concerns. This will tap into your intuition, which is that wise part of you that knows and has answers.

Your inner guide often helps heal pain, brings in loving messages, or tells you your next best step to take. Your guide may also bring a special gift. Sometimes, you might choose a favorite animal that visits and offers comfort and healing in your safe place. It's up to you. Being open and playful to whoever shows up is part of the journey. We have two magical adventures ahead. Try them both.

Meeting Your Inner Guide or Magical Wizard

Make sure you are comfortable, either sitting or lying down. Let go of any tension or stress in any part of your body. If you will, please close your eyes. Let's begin with a few deep breaths in and out. As you breathe in slowly through your nose, imagine that you are filling up a balloon on the count of 1….2….3. Now breathe out slowly through your mouth, and now breathe in 1…2…3. Than let it out…1…2…3. Let's do this a few more times on your own, 1, 2, 3…filling up with peace and calm. Now breathe out, 1, 2, 3 letting go of tension. Keep counting and breathing a few more times, counting to yourself. (Pause 10 seconds)

That's great. Now let go of counting and just breathe normally. Beautiful. Now let's imagine a white light of healing and comfort coming in from above. Or, it can be any color that you wish. (Pause briefly) Let's imagine that this loving light begins flowing into your crown from the top of your head, moving down your face, your ears, your neck, moving into your shoulders. This loving light bathes your chest and tummy, your arms, and legs, all the way down to your toes. All is well, letting go of tension. And now a special light comes back up from your toes, and travels to your heart, and expands outward surrounding you in total loving light. (Pause briefly)

On the count of 3, you will drift even further into total peace, feeling even more relaxed. 1… 2… and 3. (Pause briefly) Allow yourself to get a sense of stepping into a path. And this pathway will be leading you to your very own safe space…a place where you may invite your inner guide. So, keep moving and taking in the scenery and beauty. We are inviting only positive images and scenes. (Pause briefly)

Okay. Now you have arrived just outside your special place. See a colorful door and turn the knob to go inside. (Pause briefly) What do you see? (Pause briefly) What do you hear? (Pause briefly) Smell? How does it feel to be in your special place of love, acceptance, and peace? (Pause briefly) You may want to prepare this place so that you may invite your Inner Guide or Magical Wizard to come and join you. (Pause briefly) Now, find a place to sit or rest in your safe place.

That's great. Now get ready for your special visitor... A beautiful being, your special guide is now coming toward you with love. (Pause 20 seconds) ... What does your special guide or wizard look like? (Pause 10 seconds) So welcome this loving being, who is here to help you. Feel the love that your guide has for you.... take it all in. (Pause 20 seconds.) Your guide is here to help you, so ask your guide what would be helpful for you to know? I will be quiet for a bit, as you share this time connecting with your special guide. (Pause 30 seconds) That's great. Do you want to know anything else from your guide? Go ahead and ask and listen to the message. (Pause 30 seconds) Know that sometimes you may not get answers right away. Other times, they may show up at a later time, and that's fine, too. (Pause briefly).

Now, say thank you to your inner guide and know that you will take this love and guidance into your day or evening. (Pause 20 seconds) Allow your inner guide to go or stay in your safe place. In a few moments, it will be time for you to make your way back ... Know that you may return to your safe place and visit with your special guide at any time. But now, it is time to leave this place.

As you make your way back, you notice something special ...just for you... It's a gift to remind you of your strength and courage... Lean down and pick it up. What is it? (Pause 20 seconds) Bring that gift back with you into your present life...feeling grateful. (Pause 10 seconds)

Now let's step back along a pathway leading to your heart. ...Coming back... easily...being aware now of your body resting or sitting... see a light of peace now filling up your body with new energy of healing and love. (Pause briefly.) Now, feel yourself back in this room again...wiggle your hands and feet, if you can. Coming back feeling totally alert. Take 2 deep breaths in and out. When you're ready, open your eyes.

Cool Tips to Know

Meeting your Inner Guide or Magical Wizard is often a fun experience. Children have been comforted by what their guides tell them. You might be, too. One child was told to feel braver for an upcoming medical test and that his guide would be there with him. Another child said her inner guide was a loving angel who was there to protect her.

The figure who appears may also be a grandparent or someone else who may no longer be alive. Share what you see with your mom or dad, or another caregiver. All is okay, as you are bringing in a loving guide who only wants the very best for you and is there to help and support you. Sometimes a guide does not appear, and that's okay, too. Your special guide or wizard will appear when he or she is ready. You can try again at another time.

You may also see a favorite animal, pet, or stuffed toy and that's fine, too. In fact, you can do a similar imagery adventure with a favorite wise animal guide. It can be so easy to share things with a favorite pet or stuffed animal. It might be easier sharing your troubles with an animal friend. Once more, your parent will read this to you very slowly, when you're ready.

Meeting a Wise Animal Guide

Let's get comfortable by sitting up straight or lying down with your hands in your lap or by your sides. Let go of any tension. If you want, please close your eyes. Now breathe in slowly on the count of 3. As you breathe in slowly through your nose, imagine that you are filling up a balloon, deep in your belly… on the count of 3 breathe in 1….2….3. Now breathe out slowly through your mouth 1…2…3. Let's do this a few more times on your own, filling up with peace and calm, and letting go of stress and tension. (Pause 10 seconds) That's great. You may let go of counting now and just breathe normally again.

Now let's imagine a beautiful light of healing and comfort. Take a few moments to let go of any tension that is in any part of your body with this healing light of love. (Pause briefly) And magically, let's travel and visit your safe place. Go there now…(Pause briefly) Do you see your safe space?

Good. There, inside waiting for you is your special wise animal guide. This animal or character knows what your heart needs and wants to help you solve problems. It may be an animal that you know, or a favorite pet, or a character. That's the fun part…you never know who shows up. So, be open. (Pause 20 seconds) Now spend time with your special animal guide in your safe space. Just be with your special friend. (Pause 20 seconds)

This friend wants to help. Remember that. So, when you're ready, tell your animal friend your problem and ask for advice. I will be quiet now so you may talk to your friend. (Pause 20 seconds) Take your time and ask whatever else you need for better understanding. (Pause 20 seconds) Now thank your wise animal guide for helping you. (Pause briefly)

It's time now to leave your special place. Know that you may return at any time to be with your wise friend. (Pause briefly) Take back with you the love or guidance that you gained from your Wise Animal Guide and say thank you. (Pause 10) So, now it's time to leave your special place. Take all the good that you received. See or feel a loving peace spread throughout your body, as you leave your safe space. (Pause 10 seconds) Notice yourself back in your room. Feel where you are sitting or lying down. If you can, wiggle your fingers and toes. Now take 2 deep breaths. And when you're ready, you may open your eyes. Welcome back.

Cool Tips to Remember

If an animal does not show up during your journey, which sometimes happens, try thinking of a favorite pet or a character from a book or movie. This may help. Invite that character into your safe space. Or, ask Lucy the Llama to appear, if you like.

Having a talk with a special animal can be very helpful. You might feel more powerful with an imaginary friend. Sometimes a different kind of animal may show up that may surprise you, too, like an eagle. Ask why the eagle is there and how this animal can help. Maybe it's there to protect you. So, be open to whatever appears, just as long as you feel safe. You're welcome to do this imagery with other members of your family. Have them share their journey, as well. What did each of you see or feel? What messages did you receive? Be open to how your imaginary friend may help you to heal and to feel loved and safe.

You may also draw or color what you saw or experienced. Write down your feelings in a journal and any special messages that you received. This can be helpful for your healing and be a reminder of your special journey.

CHAPTER 6

Tuning into Your Heart Star

What is beautiful and bright and lives inside of you? It's your Heart Star! It's your connection to love, peace, and wisdom. Often during my guided imagery sessions, I have people focus on their heart. It's right there in the center of your chest, shining brightly. If you don't know where that is, ask your parent to show you.

Many spiritual teachers believe the heart is full of wisdom and connected to our soul. If we listen carefully, our heart may send us messages. Scientists now seem to back this up. They have found that the brain and heart communicate with one another. Messages are being sent back and forth from the brain to the heart.

Our next guided imagery will help you tune into your heart or your body for answers. When you're scared and feel stressed, try shifting your attention away from your head and worry thoughts, and listen to your heart. Take a breath, get quiet and ask, "Heart Star, how do I feel?" Then be still and listen. You can even put your hand on your heart if this is helpful. Viewing life through your Heart Star means that you don't judge any feelings or pain in your body. You allow them to be, just as they are. You also avoid judging yourself but instead send loving messages. Remember, you're a child of the universe and VERY special.

Have your parents or other caregivers read this to you.

Heart Star: How Do I Feel?

There are times when you are really upset. You may be sad, angry, or afraid, or something else is upsetting you. When you feel stressed, it is helpful to sit down and focus on your breath. Pausing and going inside may help you feel better

It's best to sit with your eyes closed. Begin some deep belly breathing, like the Balloon Breath. (Pause briefly) Breathe in on a count of three slowly, 1, 2, 3. Then breathe out slowly, 1, 2, 3. Continue on your own for a bit. (Pause 20 seconds) Pretend you are breathing in and out from your heart center in the middle your chest. You may feel tenderness or sadness in your heart, you may feel many other things in your body, like anger or tightness. Any emotions that come up are all okay. So, let's continue slow breathing in and out, feeling that you are breathing love and peace through your heart. (Pause briefly) That's great.

You are allowed to feel sad, angry, or scared. All feelings are okay. So, ask your Heart Star, "How do I feel?" (Pause 10 seconds) Next, find out where the feeling is located in your body right now. It could be in your throat or tummy area, or some other spot. Notice the feeling. (Pause 15 seconds) Now give that feeling the most loving attention that you would give to a friend or favorite pet. (Pause briefly) That's right. Send it all your love.

Keep shining your love and attention on this feeling and notice if it's beginning to lessen. (Pause briefly) It's important to know that you do not need to push away feelings. Just let them in. You are strong and will survive. (Pause briefly) So, bring in your superpowers of love and strength, and know that YOU are AMAZING. Pay loving attention to your hard feelings, and they will go away soon. Maybe they are already beginning to fade. (Pause briefly) Send more love to that spot.

Know that the more you practice this imagery and pay attention to your Heart Star and the feelings in your body, the more you will trust your gut and your heart. (Pause briefly) So now it's time to come back to the room. Take a few deep breaths, wiggle your fingers and toes, if you will. Breathe in and out once more. When you are ready, open your eyes.

Cool Tips to Know

When we honor feelings, it's much better for our health. Feelings eventually fade away, especially if we send the tough feelings lots of love. When doing this imagery, sometimes you will want to ask your Heart Star what you need to do to feel better, but you might not receive an answer right then. Don't worry; you might receive a wise message later. The answer will come in its own time.

Follow your Heart Star and honor your feelings. This benefits your health and happiness because you'll be more aware of what you need at the moment. By paying attention and honoring all feelings with love, you are kinder toward yourself.

The next meditation is called *Loving Kindness*, which begins in your heart. Although I have adapted it for you, this meditation has been practiced for centuries. It helps you open up to love. Have you ever felt special kindness or love from a friend? Have you noticed how good it feels? When we share kindness and love for others, it expands. Begin with love for yourself, and then spread it to others.

Have your parents or other caregivers read this to you, as you open up to *Loving Kindness*.

Loving Kindness Meditation

Sit up straight or lie down with your hands at your sides or in your lap. Get comfortable and close your eyes. Take in several deep belly breaths for calm. Think of the Balloon Breath, filling up with air deeply and slowly into your belly, on a count of 3. First breathe out, then breathe in–1, 2, 3.

Then breathing out slowly through your nose, 1, 2, 3. Do this one more time on your own filling up like a balloon.

Now breathe normally again. No need to count. Feel as though you are breathing in and out from your heart space or Heart Star very slowly. Breathe in and out from your Heart Space a few more times. (Pause 10 seconds)

Now, I will be saying loving kindness phrases and you will repeat these words silently to yourself, At the same time, sending love to your Heart Star. Okay? Here we go.

- *May I be happy.*
- *May I be healthy.*
- *May I be safe.*

Try it again. I'll say it first, then you repeat it to yourself silently.

- *May I be happy.*
- *May I be healthy.*
- *May I be safe*

Then, send this loving kindness to someone who has given you lots of love. Maybe it's a parent or grandparent, or special person. Then say these words silently to yourself. Feel your heart expand to your loved one. Remember to repeat these Loving Kindness phrases to yourself in silence.

- *May you be happy.*
- *May you be healthy.*
- *May you be safe*

Now, think of someone that made you angry, maybe it's someone at your school, or in your neighborhood, and say these words. This may be hard but do your best.

- *May you be happy.*

- *May you be healthy.*
- *May you be safe.*

Then, send this loving kindness phrase to someone in your school or your neighborhood, or another part of town, who is hurting and needs love. Feel both of your hearts surrounded by light and love. Tell this person…

- *May you be happy.*
- *May you be healthy.*
- *May you be safe. (Pause 10 seconds)*

Now, feel all the love that you have sent to others being returned. Stay with this feeling of light and love as it grows and expands your heart. (Pause 20 seconds) Stay with this feeling a little longer connecting to all living beings, sending love and joy. (Pause 20 seconds.) After a little while, you may open your eyes… Carry this kindness throughout your day. On this day or any day, spread loving kindness to yourself and others.

Cool Tips to Know

When we love ourselves first and then spread love to others, it comes back to us even bigger and brighter. We can spread so much love to our family and friends. Always remember to start from a loving place within yourself first.

Tuning into Your Heart Star

You carry so much wisdom within. Keep tuning in to your heart when you feel fear or stress. Allow love in. Remember to go inside and ask your heart and your special guide what you need. Answers will come to you from a place of love. When you have flashes of insight from your heart or tummy area, that's probably your inner superpower, and it's important to pay attention. Our inner healer brings us to the truth. It just feels right. Lucy the Llama is here to remind us to look into our hearts for guidance. Let love lead the way. Follow your heart, and it will always lead you in the right direction to follow your dreams and be happy.

CHAPTER 7

Superpower Healing to Reduce Pain

Ready to launch more of your inner healer and your SUPER-POWER? You're connected to a vast and wonderful source of energy. When we tap into this inner power, we help heal our mind and body. There have been many scientists studying how guided imagery can aid healing for health and pain relief. For children, we know it can speed healing after operations. In a different study, kids who had lots of stomach problems were helped with imagery. We also know it can help reduce symptoms and boost healing from cancer treatment, diabetes, heart problems, and so much more.

This next healing adventure will take you up and away from your pain in a hot air balloon. This may be a great way to release anything that you don't like. You'll be able to let go of fear and pain. Let's call on your healing superpower as we take off into the big blue sky.

Hot Air Balloon Ride

Let's escape your pain and discomfort. Ready to hop on board a big hot air balloon for a fun ride? Make sure you're in a comfortable position sitting up straight in a chair, with your hands in your lap or lying down with your arms by your sides. Take a few deep breaths in and out. Now close your eyes and let's begin to let go of any tension and pain. Take a deep breath in and think "Love." Let your breath out slowly and think "Free." Do this a couple of more times… deep breathing, just like that. (Pause 15 seconds) Think "Love" as you take a breath in, then think "Free" as you let your air out. (Pause 10 seconds) Beautiful. Now on the count of 3, you will be so very relaxed. Ready? 1, 2, 3. (Pause briefly). Now you are so very calm and peaceful, so deeply relaxed… (Pause briefly) Imagine that you are in your safe place. It's your very own, and it can be by the ocean, or in a cozy cave, or anyplace that makes you feel loved and safe. (Pause 10 seconds) That's great.

Right outside your safe place, you notice a big hot air balloon. It's so colorful, and it's ready to lift off with you in it. Notice the air from the balloon and any sounds. (Pause briefly) Climb up the stairs and into the basket. If you need help from a special friend or guide, that's fine. (Pause briefly) They are with you now, safe inside the basket. You're told that for the hot air balloon to take off, you must release all stress, worry, pain, and discomfort. So, you dig inside and start throwing things overboard. Grab some junk and let it go…. Each time you do that, the balloon goes up a little at a time. (Pause briefly) Keep going. Take away that pain, that fear, and keep throwing it overboard. (Pause briefly) That's great. Now the balloon is light enough and it floats gently, up and away into the big blue sky. (Pause briefly)

You feel so much better during your magical balloon ride. What do you see and hear? Breathe in joy. Let go of pain and sadness. Keep doing that. (Pause briefly) That's great. As you float around, watch the clouds above and the ground below. What do you see? What do you feel? Wave goodbye to all those feelings going away. Keep breathing and saying to yourself, silently," I am happy, and I am free." (Pause briefly) Stay here for a little bit longer enjoying the ride. And I will be quiet. (Pause 20 seconds) Now it's time to return, but you can come back to your hot air balloon anytime to release worry and pain, and to feel better and free. (Pause 10 seconds)

For now, it's time to return to your room. Make sure you bring back the feelings of joy, lightness, and fun with you. You're safe and so very loved. Now, returning to your room where you began. Notice where you are sitting or lying down. Take a few deep breaths in and out. (Pause briefly) If you can, wiggle your fingers and toes. Feel yourself back in the room. And when you are ready, open your eyes.

Children like you have enjoyed this balloon ride for releasing our troubles and discomfort. You are so much stronger than the pain in your body. Imagery can help us escape into a place of love and healing when we need it most. Our next imagery uses healing water to provide comfort and soothing relief

Healing Water Journey

Relax and get into a comfortable position, sitting up straight or lying down, with your hands in your lap or lying down. Now take four deep breaths in and out. Remember to breathe in on a count of three, 1, 2, 3. Then breathe out 1, 2, 3. Do this a few more times (Pause for 10 seconds.) Now let go and breathe normally.

As you breathe in, feel you are breathing in light and peace, and letting go of tension, stress and pain... Continue to breathe lovingly, as you imagine a white healing light. Feel a glowing light coming from your heart and it grows so large, that it wraps you in a loving light ... providing you with total peace, safety and love. (Pause)

Imagine yourself now in a beautiful forest, and you are walking in the woods... Notice the different sights and sounds, and smells. (Pause) Take in this beauty. (Pause) As you walk along, you hear the sound of water and come to a stream. Next to the stream sits a box that will float. This is a box where you can put away anything you'd like to be free of for now. Put in all of your worries and any struggles in that box. After you have filled the box, close it, put it in the water, and watch as it disappears downstream.

Walk until the stream widens and forms a private healing pool. Let the water be the perfect color and temperature. There is a sandy place to rest your head. You can take off all of your clothes or be in a bathing suit. A fluffy towel and robe lie ready for you.

As you gently go into the water notice its special healing power. If you would like, allow the healing water to go into your skin, into your muscles, even into the cells. Feel the healing action of the water washing away tension. This energy pores into your skin...all of that healing liquid comes rushing into your cells of your body and into all of your energy channels. And it's cleansing and renewing your body. The healing rushes over your head and face, into your neck and shoulders, into your arms, hands, into your stomach and chest, and your back. This loving energy pours into your legs and feet ... so that your body is glowing with beautiful bright healing energy. (Pause.) It's renewing every cell of your body. You are super charged...with this beautiful bright healing love. (Pause)

This special healing moves into your internal body parts, like your stomach and heart. Take your time. (Pause) Release anything that you no longer need and let the stream carry it away, and be revitalized by this light energy of the healing water.

Feel this water wash over any fears or worry. As you let go, give your burdens away and instead be filled with love and peace. You are so very loved. Even your tiny cells feel this new energy of compassion, love, and healing. So keep focusing on what you most love and say thank you. For being thankful is the best way to receive more love and healing. You are loved and accepted as you are...all is well and will be well.

So now you get ready to leave the stream ... You are bringing back with you all of this loving energy that will continue to work its magic as long as necessary. So you gently climb out of the healing pool. You are drying off and getting dressed again. (Pause) You are walking out of the woods back into your heart ... keeping that feeling and expansion of love and compassion for yourself and others. When you are ready come back into this room on the count of 3. Here we go. 3 ... Wiggle your fingers and toes. 2...Coming back now totally refreshed and 1...totally energized and alert. When you are ready, open your eyes.

Our next imagery, *Heal Your Body* has to do with sending healing energy to every part and tiny cell of your body. Remember that you are a miracle. There are so many wonderful cells in your body. We can send messages to our body that can aid healing, and that's what this next imagery journey is all about. Please don't feel stupid talking to your cells and your body. Hey, I will let you in on a little secret. No one is listening, but you. And, you can tell your body whatever you want, so send it nice, helpful, and healing messages. In this *Heal Your Body* adventure, you're telling your body that you want healing, comfort, and peace. Send loving messages to each cell to feel healthy and grow strong, as well. The more we take this same healing journey, the quicker our body might heal.

Heal Your Body

Find a quiet place and settle in. Either lying down or sitting in a chair, get comfortable now. Close your eyes, if you will. Take a few deep breaths in, filling up from your belly slowly, 1, 2, 3. Then let your air out very slowly. Do that 2 more times. (Pause briefly) Take a moment now to go through your entire body and if there is any tension or tightness, just let it all go. (Pause briefly)

See a white light coming up from your feet, relaxing every part of your body as it slowly, peacefully moves up, soothing any remaining tension through your legs, arms, back, shoulders—all the way up to your head, scalp, face, eyes, and tongue—totally releasing all tightness or stress with this healing light. (Pause briefly)

As it floats up through your heart, let yourself be surrounded by this light of love and peace. Let yourself float ... down ... down ... down ... within your heart to that wonderful place safe within you ... that is filled with peace. You can recall this state ... or allow yourself to go even deeper ... whenever you wish ... Simply by going inside ... and saying the words ...I am loved, I am safe, I am at peace. (Pause briefly)

As you relax, imagine yourself moving down 3 steps. With each step, you become more relaxed. 3...2... and 1... All the way down now, totally relaxed... You are open to new ideas, down on that bottom step. (Pause 10 seconds)

Now imagine a place that makes you feel safe and at peace. It can be by an ocean, with aqua blue water and white sand, or in a beautiful meadow, with a rainbow of flowers, or it can be your very own safe place. Whatever place you choose, it will be just right for you. Imagine what it feels like. What sounds do you hear...being in your special place...or smell...? What beauty do you see? Allow a feeling of total love and getting away from it all. This place makes you feel safe and loved. (Pause briefly) Now imagine finding a place to sit. You can choose anything you want... a big soft chair, or a cozy blanket. This is your place. Let yourself rest in your space of love and healing. (Pause 30 seconds)

You are now so very relaxed, and as you relax more and more deeply, you realize the power of your mind and body. A glowing light of healing comes from the center of your being and surrounds you in pure white light or any color that you choose, bathing every cell of your body with perfect healing and relaxation. Realize that you, with your superpower, are in charge of every cell in your body. And you're now telling millions of cells to heal. Say to them, "Heal, heal, heal." (Pause 20 seconds.)

Realize that everything is going to be just fine because you are in charge of your body and you have told your body to heal properly, easily, safely, quickly. You now tell all cells in your body to heal. You are at peace. Your body is healing light and energy, now and always. Say these phrases to yourself,

- *I am so happy to feel so much better.*
- *I am so happy to feel safe.*
- *I am so happy to heal and feel loved.*

If it's time for sleep, you will go into a very deep and healing rest, and you will ignore the rest of this message. And if it's time to wake up…you may now return to your room…feel your body where you are sitting or lying down. Now wiggle your fingers and toes. Take 2 deep breaths…when you are ready, open your eyes.

This next imagery involves a Magical Healing Glove. It may help you need less pain medicine. A lot of children and teens like this imagery because it's a way to reduce pain without having to take more medication. It can be used for short-term pain relief following surgery or injury.

Magical Healing Glove

Let's go on a healing journey to discover how we may help reduce pain. Get comfortable lying down or sitting in a chair. Now close your eyes and let's take some deep breaths. Breathe into your belly on the count of 3, like you're filling up a balloon, 1, 2, 3. Then, let it out through your mouth 1, 2, 3. That's great. Do a few more breaths like that deep and slow. (Pause 10 seconds)

Beautiful. As you take in more breaths peacefully in and out, see a white light coming from above your head and now it gently moves down through your body, letting go of tension, through your head, your neck, and shoulders, your arms, chest, and belly, on through your legs into your feet and out through the ground. That's great. You are so relaxed listening to your breathing in and out. (Pause briefly) Now we're going to go even deeper on the count of 3, so very relaxed…1, 2, 3. (Pause briefly) very calm and at peace.

Now imagine that there's a dreamy, glowing bucket of cooling pain relief, like a liquid energy of magical healing. It can be blue, or any color that you choose. Imagine placing one hand in the cooling liquid light which will numb your hand. See it… Swish your hand around the numbing solution. (Pause briefly)

What does it feel like? (Pause briefly) You notice your hand now is becoming numb. Magically, it is spreading up your arm, taking all pain away. It feels like a glove of pure cooling comfort. That's right…feel it spreading to any part of your body that is in pain.

Take that magical glove of comfort and place it on the part of your body that is in pain. That's great...like magic, it is taking away your pain. Feel how much better you feel...you are more comfortable and relaxed. Stay with that spot for a little while longer. (Pause 10 seconds)

If there is another spot that needs healing, move your magical glove to that place as well or stay in that original spot. It's so comforting. You are feeling so much better...it is so soothing and feels like being wrapped in a blanket of peace. (Pause 20 seconds)

Now you may bring your hand and magical glove down by your side again... Know you may always call on your magical glove and liquid energy for healing at any time for any discomfort or pain. That's right. Now that you feel less pain and more healing take this comfort with you throughout your day. (Pause briefly) When you are ready, begin returning to your room. Take a few deep breaths in. Becoming aware of your body, as it is lying down or sitting. When ready, open your eyes. Feeling so much better. Welcome back.

It's amazing how powerful your mind and body can be when we go on healing journeys and find our superpowers. Our next exercise is called *Turning Down Pain*. Using your imagination, you use your superpower to turn down pain and release healing light. You can do this at any time that you need to feel less pain.

In this journey, you're going to connect to a magical crystal knob. So, when you turn it a certain way, it will provide pain relief. Have your mom or dad or other caregiver show you what that may look like, using a pretend knob in the air. See that your hand is surrounding a sparkling and colorful crystal knob. As you turn the knob in a certain direction, it reduces the pain. Turn the knob one way, and then the other way. Okay, now you're ready.

Turning Up Comfort

If you will, imagine two sparkling, colorful crystal knobs. Do you see them? They can be any color that you want. Your favorite colors. You may turn the glittering magical knobs in either direction. In your mind, you are going to turn down discomfort with the knob on your left from 10 to zero. And turn the knob on the right way up for more comfort, so by the time you reach an 8 or 10, you're going to feel so much better. So, get ready to turn up comfort. This is one of your superpowers.

Let's get more relaxed now. Sitting up straight in a chair or in a bed. Let your hands rest in your lap or by your sides, if lying down. Now close your eyes and take a few deep breaths in and out. Fill up your breath deep into your belly. Fill up with air on the count of 3…1, 2, 3. Hold it. Then breathe out…1, 2, 3. Do this a few more times on your own on the count of 3. (Pause 10 seconds) Now let go of counting.

See a beautiful light pouring into the top of your head. It makes you feel loved, calmer, and relaxed, as it spreads throughout your body. This loving light flows in from above your head… all the way from your head, into your neck and shoulders, down through your tummy area, hips, and then down into your legs, to your feet, and let it all go to the ground… and give it to Mother Earth.

Then this loving light comes back to your heart space or Heart Star and surrounds you with love and light. (Pause 10 seconds) On the count of 3, you will feel even more relaxed and at peace…1, 2, 3. (Pause 10 seconds) We are now going to use a superpower. This will help lower any pain or discomfort in your body and replace it with soothing love and healing.

Imagine two sparkling crystal knobs again. They can be any color that you choose. (Pause briefly) You will turn down one crystal knob to help be free of any discomfort At the same time, we are going turn the comfort knob on our right way up, so we feel more comfort and soothing.

So, let's try that now… See the crystal knobs being turned so that your pain is magically being released. The discomfort is going away and your comfort level is going up and up. You're doing great. Let's try that one more time. Turn the knobs even more to lessen pain on one side, then bring on healing and comfort… Beautiful. Wow, you are doing so well…feel this shower of glittering light and love from above spreading over your entire body. The pain is fading away, and now you feel more love, and healing…That's great.

Know you may use these crystal knobs to turn down pain and increase comfort at any time. So, now that you are feeling better, we will take this comforting energy of love and healing and soothing back with us. (Pause briefly)

Enjoy the showering of glittering light of love once more. (Pause 15 seconds) Take a few deep breaths in. (Pause briefly) When you are ready, begin returning to the room where we started this journey. Become aware of your body where it is lying down or sitting. When ready, open your eyes and you will feel so much better with more calm and comfort.

Cool Tips to Remember

If you don't see something in your mind at first, that's fine. You can repeat this journey. If you don't remember the imagery or what you felt, that's fine too. All is well, even if you fall asleep. It will still reach your deeper mind and inner healer to feel more comfort and peace.

These journeys will become easier for you to enjoy the more you do them. It's like building a muscle to make you big and strong. You're waking up your inner superpower, which is ready to help you at any time. Have fun mixing up the different imagery adventures. Continue to use your favorites at any time for special love and healing.

CHAPTER 8

Sleepytime Dreams for Children

Are you sleeping soundly? Do you wish it was easier to fall asleep? Sleep can be a challenge to many children and adults, especially during a hospital visit or when you don't feel well. Doctors who treat children report that more than one third have sleep concerns. Poor sleep early in childhood may be linked to learning and behavior challenges, too, so it's important that you get a good night's rest.

Our next adventure will help you fall asleep and stay asleep. Get ready to feel loved, safe, and protected by your dream fairy. Since sleep is so vital for repairing young minds and bodies, use this imagery to help you sleep more soundly. It is recommended for children between the ages of three and six. We also have a version of *Sleepytime Dreams* for ages seven to twelve.

Sleepytime Dreams
(Ages 3 to 6)

Get comfortable in your bed or where you are sitting or resting. Take a few breaths in and out. (Pause briefly) Breathe in slowly…now breathe out… I am happy that you are lying down so that special fairy dust can wrap you up in a soft and safe cocoon. Snuggle into your space little caterpillar. And rest my little butterfly, flutter to a soft area… and rest peacefully.

Close your eyes and let your body float like a balloon. Feel warm and safe in your soothing space…take a deep breath…let your belly fill with air and rise and fall, then blow out like a big blowfish…breathe out…let your body melt…calm down…and fill your body with air once more, then let it out and let my loving fairy dust…bring you to a warm, safe, place, filled with love and comfort. (Pause briefly)

Yawn… You are safe and cozy…my fairy dream dust of love flows with warmth throughout each part of your body. Let your arms sink into your resting place. Feel your fingers and hands get heavy and sleepy…now your legs…your feet and toes…feel heavy, warm, and relaxed, as your tummy, back, and neck melt into your bed or another surface. Let go…. Let all parts of your lovely body, your face, eyes, and mouth let go…your mind relax. Let them rest now and go into sleepytime dreams… (Pause 10 seconds)

Feel your heart open and expand as you rest and relax…ready for a sleepytime dream. Your eyelids feel heavy and calm and relaxed. Your body is still, and your eyes are closed. See a movie in your mind, as colorful light floats above your head…your favorite color…you feel warm, safe, and loved. Dream about this light…a big beautiful bubble, your favorite color covers you... like a soft blanket. Calm down and float. You are a butterfly, floating up, up and away. (Pause briefly) You can slow down, stop, or land softly. (Pause briefly) Enjoy a gentle, smooth ride as the breeze lifts you up to the big blue sky with many soft, fluffy clouds. There are many, many clouds... as you relax.

You land on one of the clouds. It's a safe place to rest. So, you stretch out a little more... lying back down with your soft blanket. Feel the warmth of the sun... the soft breeze, as you float up and away... the cloud gently rocks you back and forth, back and forth... safe and loved. The fresh scent of flowers fills the air as you relax and rest. Only sweet dreams and thoughts fill your mind. You feel warm, safe and loved... where you are... rest... safe and cozy, rocking back and forth, back and forth, back and forth. "I feel loved, I feel safe, I feel peaceful. ...I am loved, I am safe, I am peaceful..." (Pause briefly)

Feel the warmth of the sun... a soft breeze on your face, as you rest on your cloud. You are happily floating on your cloud... your dream fairy rocks you back and forth, back and forth, back and forth... rest my sweet angel, rest.

Cool Tips to Remember

Sleepytime Dreams is a guided imagery program for young children that can be used for naps and at bedtime. Having been tested at four different preschools and early childhood programs before launching nationwide, the imagery works for even difficult nappers. At home, parents report that *Sleepytime Dreams* helps children fall asleep quicker and stay asleep longer.

Older children also have trouble sleeping. You're under so much pressure with homework, sports, music lessons, not to mention all of the devices wanting your attention. With video games and texting friends, you may be so revved up at night that you have trouble letting go and allowing your body to rest. Many adults have this problem, too.

Remember this when you have trouble going or staying asleep. Try a few deep breathing exercises that you learned in earlier chapters to help you release and let go. See if that helps you relax. Or, you may find this guided imagery, *Sleepytime Dreams* for ages seven to twelve, helpful, as well. At first, it might be easier to have someone guide you into deep relaxation. Once you learn these relaxation techniques, then you can do them on your own.

Sleepytime Dreams
(Ages 7 to 12)

Take a moment to make sure that you are in a comfortable spot away from anything that could disturb you. This is your time to relax and unwind. Get comfortable now. Lie down on your bed or another surface, with your arms at your sides loose and limp. Please close your eyes and go inside. Just let go for now. Any outside noises from now on will make you feel even more relaxed.

First, let's focus on your breathing. I want you to breathe in a special way. You begin to relax tension as you breathe in on the count of 3, 1, 2, 3. Then let it out, 1, 2, 3. Once more breathe in peace 1, 2, 3. Then release your breath on 3...

Continue breathing in and out slowly, and gently. As you release all tension in your mind and body, moment by moment, you will find that you will free yourself from any thoughts of stress and worry of the day. Just let it all go for this peaceful time for you. (Pause 10 seconds)

Now, let yourself imagine a healing light above your head. (Pause 5 seconds) Let this glowing light become stronger and stronger as it is absorbed through the top of your head. You will be surprised and amazed that with each breath; you are becoming soft and more relaxed.

Feel the light energy flow into your head and scalp. Let go of any tension around your eyes. Let your jaw relax by allowing your mouth to be slightly open and let your tongue relax. Just let go. Even your ears are becoming relaxed. Relax your cheeks and any muscles in your face. Just release and let go. Continue this relaxation. Enjoy the peace and calm that you feel. (Pause 10 seconds)

Now let's focus on your neck. Allow that warm glow of relaxation to flow down into your shoulders. How wonderful your body feels as it melts into softness. Deeper and deeper into total peace and relaxation. Turn your attention to both arms. They feel heavy, sinking deeper. They become totally loose and limp, all the way down into your fingertips. Release and let go. (Pause 10 seconds)

Let's bring your awareness to the center of your being around your belly button. Feel how this area of your body and chest gently rises and falls as you breathe. The loving light soothes every organ. You can feel the release, as all muscles go limp and heavy, deeper and deeper. (Pause 10 seconds)

Spread this relaxation through the lower part of your body. Feel this relaxation flow into your legs and feet into your toes. Just release and let go. (Pause 20 seconds)

Now we are going to relax your mind as well as your body. Picture a helium balloon. We are going to put in that balloon any thoughts that upset you. So now just let go of any upsetting thoughts and place them in the balloon. See the balloon lift off, up, up, and away. (Pause) You are now resting. Feel your body so soft and at peace… drifting even further into a deep, restful sleep counting down from 3… 2… 1…

You are now in your safe and cozy space, surrounded by a blanket of love, warmth, and total peace. You are wrapped in a healing cocoon of protective light… and this shield of loving energy makes you feel loved, safe and protected. You may even repeat this phrase to yourself but not out loud:

- *I am loved. (Pause briefly)*
- *I am safe. (Pause briefly)*
- *I am at peace. (Pause 10 seconds)*

Sleepytime Dreams for Children

Now as you are drifting off into a peaceful and restful sleep, you will stay asleep until it's time to wake up. Feel this beautiful, glowing energy in your heart, and as it expands, it is wrapping you in total love. You will only experience restful, peaceful dreams…for you are very special and need this precious time to relax and restore…rest my sweet angel…rest.

Cool Tips to Remember

I know what it's like not getting the rest needed. For years, I suffered from too little sleep, only three or four hours per night. With that little sleep, it's hard on your body and well-being. Guided imagery, along with the breathing exercises, has allowed my worries to drift away, and given me a deep and restful sleep.

And now, I'm giving this gift to you. The deep breathing and release of stress, tension, and worry will help you get the rest you need. If you continue having trouble with worrisome thoughts, consider writing in a worry notebook. Keep it by your bed, so you can write down your thoughts, and then let them go.

Inner Power NOW is always there for you to explore, whether it's breath work, escaping pain by lifting off in a hot air balloon or using the crystal knob to turn down discomfort. These healing journeys are waiting and available to you. Once you practice enough, you'll be able to imagine healing images on your own. Remember to go to your safe place. Have an animal friend or magical wizard come to visit. Ask questions to receive advice and help. Please continue calling on your superpower that is so strong and amazing and connected to your wise self. My recordings are also there for you to help in your healing journeys.

Lucy Llama and I are happy and grateful that you've taken this journey with us. You are so loved and special. We hope you'll continue to use imagery when times are tough, you're in pain, or you feel unsafe or alone. You have a wonderful power within you. Just remember to open your Heart Star and let your light shine.

The next chapters are geared for older teens and adults.

Part 3

For Teens, Parents, and Caregivers

CHAPTER 9

Inner Power NOW for Teens

Thank you for joining me on this healing journey! Hopefully, you've had a chance to experience some of the earlier sessions, like the breathing tips (Chapter 1) and guided imagery like *Discover Your Safe Place* (Chapter 4) *Loving kindness Meditation* (Chapter 6) and using your imagination for healing and pain control. (Chapter 7.)

As teenagers, you may see *Inner Power NOW* as entirely unrelated to your busy lives. You might be surprised at how you could benefit by relaxing with breath work, meditation, and guided imagery. Here are a few ways:
- Relieves stress and anxiety
- Aids healing, backed by thousands of studies in adults, teens, and children
- Improves self-esteem and self-love
- Supports healthy emotional development
- Enhances focus and concentration

When we go within through meditation, guided imagery, and being mindful, we lower the stress hormone cortisol. We also learn to become more of a witness to the mind. Much of the chatter in our heads is just that—chatter, which is *not* reality. It's worry, anxiety, and fearful projection. Meditation and guided imagery can help you to become more aware of your thoughts and view them objectively without getting caught up in the fear or worry.

Guided meditations are growing in popularity in education. Many public and private schools are providing mindfulness exercises and teaching meditation to students and teachers. The reason is that children, especially teens, are facing enormous pressure in and out of school.

We all face stress but being stressed-out is optional. Stress is really a form of fear, and normally shows up when you take a test or give a speech. Studies reveal that when people *expect* stress, they're actually less stressed. Instead of letting stress get the best of us, as when giving a speech, replace the fear (stress) with excitement. Tell yourself you're excited instead of stressed.

It's helpful to remember that you're resilient. When life throws you a few curve balls, have confidence that you'll be able to handle it. Meditation and guided imagery will help you better cope with life. In time, you'll open the more compassionate and creative parts of your brain.

One aspect that's vital to your happiness is compassion toward yourself. Do you ever beat yourself up by thinking you're not good enough, smart enough, pretty enough, or thin enough? You can learn to manage that inner critic by refusing to listen when it starts raging. Positive psychologists (those who study how humans can live fulfilling, happy lives) recommend that you name your inner critic right away. Also, look for the positive in yourself and others, while refusing to see only the negative. If all else fails, consider placing a large piece of black tape over your inner critic's mouth. You can also inform your inner critic that you want a more loving coach.

I have a guided imagery that can help you do that. It's called *Inner Power Loving Coach*. This meditation may be helpful to you, as well as to your parents. It's a way to connect with your wise eternal self. This higher self is always there to guide and love you and communicate with you in unique ways. You may have already noticed the connection. Maybe you've received a flash of intuition, a hunch in your gut, such as thinking about a friend who then calls you a minute later or coming across a book or blog post that contains the perfect information you need. Not only does the inner critic or your ego live in your mind, but at a deeper level, so lies your inner guide, which some call "The Witness" or "Observer." That's your wise self.

If you don't have someone who can read this to you, visit our website, InnerPowerMindset.com to listen to the audio. The best way to experience my guided imagery is through the audio programs created for this book.

Inner Power Loving Coach

Relax and get into a comfortable position, sitting up straight with your hands in your lap or lying down with your arms at your sides. Close your eyes. Now take 4 deep breaths in and out. Remember to breathe in slowly 1, 2, 3. Now, release very slowly 1, 2, 3. Do this one a few more times. (Pause 20 seconds) Now let go and breathe normally, just noticing your breath.

As you breathe in, feel you are breathing in light and peace, and letting go of tension, stress, and negativity of the day. Continue to breathe lovingly, as you bring your awareness to the top of your head. Just sense or imagine a feeling of relaxation beginning to spread down from the top of your scalp like a warm, thick liquid melting away tension throughout your body.

This nurturing warmth releases all tension and pain. Your body feels heavier and heavier. Relax more and more deeply with each breath. Sink into total serenity. As your body relaxes, your mind becomes more relaxed, and your thoughts seem to grow lighter. You are slipping further into stillness and peace. Notice how good it feels to be so gently embraced. Feel a glowing light coming from your heart. Feel that center... and it grows so large that it wraps you in a beautiful cocoon of protective light...providing you with total peace, safety, and love.

I'd like you to imagine this huge column of light and love pouring from above into your heart and surrounding you all around. This energy pours into your skin...all of that white light comes rushing into the cells of your body and your energy channels. And it's cleansing and revitalizing your body. You are supercharged...with this beautiful bright healing light. (Pause briefly)

Everywhere this light goes, it's opening up your energy and all your senses, it's allowing an opening to receive guidance from a higher place. When your energy is opened, you're more open to guidance from your higher power and higher wisdom. Feel yourself now wrapped in this protective love... let go and surrender. (Pause 30 seconds)

So now you may relax even further. Just let yourself float into the loving light of source and your wise inner self who wants to help and guide you to experience your ideal life. It knows your potential; how wonderful you truly are. It wishes you would know it too. Remember that your higher self is part of you. It loves you and wishes you only the best. (Pause briefly) You may ask any questions knowing the answers will come in the form of messages or insights later. So, if there is a burning question or answer to a problem that you need right now, ask for insight, knowing your answer will come. (Pause 30 seconds)

You may get messages from coincidences, reading something, or from your intuition. You may hear something, or you may receive insight from journaling. Any of these things will show that your wise self is connected, so I will be silent for a bit while you ask and connect for clarity. (Pause 1 minute)

Your way of life will now be more effortless because you are connected and being guided and guarded for your highest good. (Pause briefly) You surrender, knowing that you will be directed to your next best step. (Pause briefly)

Your connection with your inner power will grow more and more. You are allowing this peace and wisdom to help you create your heart's desires with all aspects of yourself working beautifully together. (Pause briefly) As you're sitting now picturing your best life, it's like a magnet being drawn to you. (Pause briefly). So sense it all right now, what you most want. (Pause for 20 seconds.)

With gratitude, place your hand over your heart. Say thank you for your blessings and lessons. (Pause 10 seconds) Your wise self and inner power are always there for you. So, continue to connect and ask for guidance. Also, you may return to this guided imagery at any time to help your connection grow and blossom.

So, welcome your deepest thoughts and heartfelt emotions and a knowing that all is well in your world. All is working out for your highest good, and you are safe. Gently bring yourself back into this room, feel where you are sitting or lying down. If you will, wiggle your fingers and toes, and when you are ready, open your eyes.

Realize that there is a wise and loving coach within your heart and ready to help, so connect with this loving source often. It is your eternal self, which is a part of you, that knows your potential and wants to help you reach your best. Be open to messages that you may receive as a flash of insight. A lot of time, this voice speaks to your heart as a flash of intuition. Some may call it the God or Christ within. You may also find journaling helpful.

Try this exercise. For five to ten minutes, allow your loving coach to write a letter to you from this higher perspective. You may be surprised by what is written. Another thing that may be helpful is tuning into messages. Keep a journal and ask questions with your writing hand. Then, write the answers using your other (non-writing) hand. Many have found this to be useful. It's a dialogue between you and your higher power or wiser self.

Who Wins—Inner Critic or Wise Self?

One more thing that I want to share before moving on to the next segment. Let's have a heart-to-heart talk about the inner critic. That's the voice in your head that may be critical or full of fear and doubt.

Completing this book and bringing it to market has been quite an inner power struggle in my own journey. Funny how that's the name of my book—*Inner Power NOW*. When I decided on this name, it was to help you and your family connect to that inner wise self and inner healer that can guide us with compassion, and provide peace and healing, and inspiration. Yet, I have to admit that on many days, both sides of me were in a huge power struggle. It was like I had one foot on the gas pedal and the other on the emergency brake. The dreamer side was up against the inner critic or the EGO that some call: "Edging God Out."

Do you ever have these moments? You're really excited, feeling good about your life, and then the doubt hits! You start to REALLY question yourself and go on a downward spiral. Finally, one day I had an epiphany. "Wow! Here I am promising the virtues of tuning into our wiser, higher self, when I am giving too much power to my EGO, with all this fear mongering." So that day, I said to my inner critic. "Thank you for sharing, but I'm not buying it!" That really felt good, so I said it again. "Thank you for sharing, but I'm not buying it!" This has become my new mantra with the inner critic.

I have learned to make peace with my EGO, asking it to be more of a loving coach and refusing to believe those negative thoughts. I need to stand strong in my beliefs with courage because I was given this vision and dream—to provide you the best tools to gain more freedom from suffering—and it's up to me to see it through. I want you and your family to feel strong, be resilient, and believe that whatever hardships you are facing today, there is a reason. It may not be fair but you will grow and learn from the experience, no matter what.

Are you with me in standing up to that doubting fearful inner critic? "Thank you for sharing, but I'm not buying it!" Now, we know the true meaning of inner power.

So…who has the power now?

Managing Test Anxiety

Taking Tests can be stressful, even among students who are very prepared. The brightest students can experience text anxiety, especially if they're perfectionists. While test taking is never fun, there are things you can do to help manage stress. You may already be doing some of these. They include:
- Get enough sleep before the exam—at least eight hours
- Prepare in advance of your test
- Be organized in your studies and make lists of what's important week to week
- Avoid distractions like video games and TV shows until tests are over

- Visualize Success—see the top score you want to make as mental imagery

I invite you to record this guided imagery on *Ace Your Test*. Read it very slowly with pausing or you're welcome to enjoy the guided meditation recording on our website.

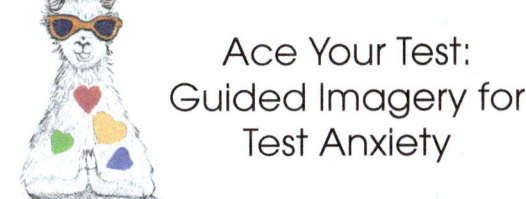

Ace Your Test: Guided Imagery for Test Anxiety

Make sure that you are seated comfortably or lying down, where you will not be disturbed. If sitting, uncross your arms and legs with your spine straight. Rest your hands in your lap. If lying down, hands by your side. And, if you will, please close your eyes and take a few slow deep breaths in, and out. This is your time for relaxation and peace.

Now we're going to breathe in a special way to bring calm and focus, like how the Navy SEALS are trained with this meditative breath. First, let your air out. Now breathe in on a count of four, 1, 2, 3, 4. Hold for four. Breathe out on a count of four….and hold for four again. One more time…take a deep breath in for four…hold it…breathe out…hold it. Now let go of counting, and just breathe normal again.

As you take a breath, feel peace coming in, and as you breathe out let go of tension. Focus on your breathing in and out for a little while. (pause for 30 seconds.)

Now do a quick scan of your body and notice any tension in any part of your body…any discomfort at all. Just release. Imagine with a wave of relaxation that pours into your head… into your scalp. Soften your eyes. Relax your jaw… Let this energy soothe your neck and shoulders…(Pause for 10 seconds)…down through your upper body…(Pause 10 seconds.) Let any remaining tension melt in your chair or into the floor.

Now that your body is more relaxed, we will let go to open up to a greater awareness. We will count down from 5 to 1 doubling your relaxation with each number.

At five your mind is opening and listening with inner ears…Four…becoming calmer …Three…you are letting go and feeling very relaxed… Two… doubling your relaxation. And One…totally relaxed and open to new ideas. (Pause)

You are now so very relaxed and focused… Just like you are when you study. Relaxed and focused. Just like you are when you take tests.

Imagine yourself studying, preparing for a test. …. The information goes into your mind easily and effortlessly… That's right.

Imagine yourself studying and retaining the information. And see how focused you are. The information just flows into your mind easily. You are so relaxed and at ease. You realize how easy it is for you to study and focus. It's that same feeling being relaxed and at ease taking a test or exam…

Whatever kind of test it is, you are able to produce the information from your mind. Your memory is excellent. Your ability to focus is excellent. (Pause.) Your study skills are great. Your test taking skills are excellent. Take a moment to feel how confident, and relaxed, knowing the right answers are there in your mind and easily flow in as you take your test… (Pause 20 seconds)

Now imagine that all of these test-taking skills are becoming more powerful day by day. (Pause 20 seconds). So relax and realize that when you take a test, you are very efficient, storing and retrieving data easily and efficiently. So relax now and realize just how powerful you are. Once more, see the high grade or score you want. Feel the pride, enthusiasm, all the great feelings. Congratulate yourself for a job well-done. You are ready for success. (Pause 10 seconds)

Successful people know that success starts before the exam... on the night before the exam... you go to bed on time. On the morning of the exam you open your eyes refreshed, alert, excited, and ready for great results. Say to yourself but not out loud:

- *"I am confident and feel strong when taking an exam." (Pause 5-10 seconds.)*
- *"I am relaxed and comfortable while taking a test" (Pause 5-10 seconds.)*

Feel the satisfaction peace and contentment of doing well on your test or exam. See the high grade or score that you want. Feel the pride, enthusiasm, all the great feelings. Congratulate yourself on a job well-done. You have aced your exam. (pause 20 seconds.)

Now it's time to bring your awareness back into this room, gently back to the space you're in…you feel energized from all that you received. (Pause 10 seconds.) Please sense where you are, sitting in your chair or lying down, as we count back from three, two and one. Feeling fully refreshed and fully alert. And when you're ready, gently open your eyes.

Here's another healing journey that will help you release the day and fall asleep easier. In it, you tense different parts of your body and then relax like a floppy stuffed animal to let go of stressful thoughts and worry. *Relax Your Body* is inspired by a well-known calming exercise called Progressive Relaxation introduced over 50 years ago. As physician and author Edmund Jacobsen said, "An anxious mind cannot exist in a relaxed body." Once you understand this relaxation exercise, you can do it on your own.

Relax Your Body:

Lie down on your bed or another surface. Get comfortable and take a couple of deep breaths in, like you are filling up a balloon on a count of 3: Filling up slowly through your nose 1, 2, 3. Now let the air out through your mouth slowly 1, 2, 3. Do this deep breathing a few more times. If you need to count to 2 because of your breathing, that's fine. (Pause 10 seconds) Beautiful. Keep breathing slowly. You no longer need to count, just breathe in and out calmly.

Now bring your attention to your body. We are going to practice letting go…feeling more soft, loose and limp. This will help you let go of stress and tension.

We are going to mention certain body parts, and I want to be sensitive to this. If you are missing a limb, like a foot or hand, then just choose another body part to focus on. We want this to be comforting to all. Let's begin with your feet first. Point your toes gently; do not strain. Now, let them go and feel soft again. Feel the difference between feeling tight and feeling soft and relaxed. Tighten your toes again, pointing them. Hold it. Now let go. Feel softer. Moving on to your legs…press your knees together and tighten your legs, and then let go of the tension…let everything become soft and loose.

Shift your attention to your belly. Pull in your belly tight…hold it, don't strain…then relax your belly and let it go soft…feel your tummy relax and notice a gentle breathing in and out. (Pause briefly) Try that one more time. Tighten your tummy. Then soften, relax, and feel the difference.

Let's move to your hands. Close your hands and make a fist, if you can… make them tight and strong…feel the tension… Now let them go. Feel the difference between tension and how it feels to be soft and relaxed. Tighten your whole arms and hands and fingers. Hold it. Now let them go. Feel that all the tension is gone, even your little pinky fingers are relaxed…all are soft. (Pause briefly)

Now, if this is okay, lift your shoulder up toward your ears and tighten. Hold it. Then let go and feel going limp and soft. Do that one more time… lift and tighten your shoulders. Now let them go and feel soft.

Let's move your attention to your face. Squeeze your eyes shut and clench your jaw and tighten all your facial muscles…then let that go… all tension. Feel the difference? One more time squeeze your face. Now let that go.

Now tighten everything in your body at once. Hold it tight. Now release, let go and soften your entire body. Go through your body and soften any tightness that remains. Let it all go. (Pause briefly) That's great. Your whole body is relaxed and calm. (Pause briefly) Feel a loving light surrounding you now in peace. (Pause briefly) Let in this healing light of comfort and peace. Love is always here ready to help us unwind and feel calmer. (Pause briefly) Now rest and allow yourself to enter a very peaceful and relaxing sleep. You can ignore the next instructions. Just drift. (Pause briefly) If it's time to be awake, come back into your room. Take a few deep breaths. When you're ready, open your eyes.

This healing journey might be helpful to you when you want to rest and can't seem to settle down. When we can let go of thoughts and tune into our body with breathing and being aware, we are then open to more love and calm.

Boosting Self Esteem and Confidence

Another helpful tool with guided imagery and meditation is building self-esteem and self-love. Too many of us take that critical voice inside too seriously. It's time to silence the voice that says we are not good enough, smart enough, or thin enough. Let's instead embrace more compassion toward ourselves and others. Throughout your day, choose things that will also make you happier. This next imagery is a confidence booster. All of us can use this in our lives from time to time, especially during difficult periods.

Empowering Self-Esteem

Get comfortable, either sitting up straight, with hands in your lap, or lying down, with hands by your side. We're going to breathe like the Navy SEALS for calm and focus. If counting to four is too difficult, then you may breathe in on the count of 3 or 2. So first breathe your air out. Now, breathe in on the count of four...1, 2, 3, 4. Pause for four... Breathe out on four... and pause for four... Great. For the next few moments, I want you to focus on your breathing in and out...just like that...breathing deep from your belly, then letting it out. (Pause briefly.)

Now, let yourself imagine a healing light that is simply glowing...about a foot above your head. Can you sense that this light has the power of special healing? Feel its healing nature ... as it soothes all thoughts of tension or stress ... providing a nurturing warmth that can be felt everywhere. Notice especially how it relaxes every muscle nerve and fiber; even your jaw and tongue are more relaxed.

Let this glowing light grow even brighter as it's absorbed by your body. Notice how good it feels to be so gently embraced... give your body permission to allow any remaining tension to flow all the way out of your body. Watch this glowing light become so large, that it wraps you in a beautiful cocoon of protective light providing you with total peace.

Now I want you to imagine that we have a magical helium balloon. And we're putting any thoughts that no longer serve you into the balloon. Let them go. As the balloon goes higher and higher, all your negative thoughts, stress, tension, and discomfort are released. (Pause briefly)

I want you to let yourself go to the most relaxing place that you can imagine—a place of peace and safety, like by an ocean or mountainside. (Pause 10 seconds) Go to this beautiful place that makes you feel calm and serene. Let yourself breathe in this beautiful, safe place. (Pause briefly) You can go to this place at any time, and it's a place full of wisdom and total serenity. (Pause briefly)

Now that you're in a peaceful place feel your heart open just a little bit more...a warm expansion of healing energy from your heart center...feel your heart expand...as you think of who you love and who loves you. (Pause 40 seconds)

Now allow anything to come into your heart... anything that you need to release. You are releasing and letting go of negative beliefs. You are wonderful and unique...and very special. All who know you realize how awesome you are. So, think of 3 things that you do better than anyone else. I'm going to give you some time to think about those things. (Pause 30 seconds) Imagine the first thing that you do well and allow yourself to feel good about that. It could be making friends, having compassion for others, doing creative work, taking part in a sport, or utilizing a special talent. See yourself doing this thing and allow yourself to feel good about it. (Pause 30 seconds) Allow a feeling of confidence to begin to grow within you. (Pause 20 seconds.)

And now think of something else—the number-two thing—that you do well. Feel this appreciation growing inside you. (Pause 30 seconds)

Now tune into the third quality or way of being that is uniquely you. Focus on that and how that quality or way of being radiates from you to others. (Pause 30 seconds)

As you continue to listen to this recording, more qualities and more things will come to mind as to how special you really are. You're wonderful. You're limitless. You have wonderful qualities that make you feel good about yourself, and you love yourself. You are kind to others and kind to yourself. Be respectful of yourself, and you avoid situations that do not honor you because you deserve to be honored and respected. You avoid negative situations and avoid negative limiting beliefs. (Pause briefly)

You also treat yourself with respect by eating right and exercising as you can, and having fun. You honor yourself as a powerful, amazing YOU. These qualities will expand even more. Others also know this to be true. (Pause 20 seconds)

Say to yourself but not out loud:

- *I love and accept myself completely as I am.*
- *I listen to my own voice and make wise decisions.*
- *I feel confident and express myself freely and easily.*
- *I take time to unwind so I can tune into my heart's desires.*

You now hold this beautiful power of light and love, this power that has always been within you. Like seeds, they will grow as they are nurtured and fed. So focus on the good that will expand. You feel this calm confidence, as you release and let go of old pain. See yourself as confident and with grace…appreciating the true essence of you. Your compassion illuminates all that you do. (Pause briefly)

Now take a moment to visualize yourself sitting in an ocean of white healing light. Come from your heart—what is it that you most want in your life right now? (Pause briefly) Your life is beautifully expanding with this energy from a loving source. (Pause 10 seconds) Imagine your life a few months from now…you're in charge and creating the life you desire. See yourself more energetic and enjoying yourself. With gratitude, place your hand over your heart, and let it all unfold by a higher loving source. Now place your hand back down again. (Pause 10 seconds)

We're going to be returning to the room where we began. Welcome your deepest thoughts and heartfelt emotions and a knowing that all is well in your world. So, as I count you back now…. Feeling refreshed and energized from all that you received…a little more aware now at 4…halfway there now at 3…take a deep breath at 2… feeling refreshed and alert now at 1. Come back into this room and when you're ready, open your eyes.

  Please know that you are unique and special. No one on this earth is quite like you. You are here to share your light, love, creativity, and gifts. When times are tough, and someone may mistreat you, say to yourself, "No matter what you say or do, I am still a worthwhile person." I learned this phrase from best-selling author and trainer Jack Canfield, and I use it myself when I feel I'm being harshly criticized or mistreated. Repeat it to yourself a few times until you feel better.

  We know that being a teen dealing with peer pressure can be especially challenging. Self-love is not a show of selfishness or weakness. It's a show of strength, especially if it helps raise your self-esteem and confidence, so you can continue to believe in and challenge yourself.

We all face failures and disappointments. Know that you will rise above even stronger. That's priceless!

In the next few chapters, I will be sharing more guided imagery and mindful techniques and tools for parents. Be open to trying these for yourself, as well.

CHAPTER 10

Inner Power NOW for Parents and Caregivers

Thank you for leading your child or teen on these healing journeys to help end suffering, so you and your family thrive. This chapter is for you parents and caregivers with guided imagery geared for adults. Some programs may also be helpful for teens.

Meditation and guided imagery can help us discover what lies in our heart, in the very soul of our being. When we let go of the mind and embrace the stillness that lives in our heart, we find more love and healing. This is where we may find our inner wisdom and superpower that is connected to God or universal source consciousness. In fact, that's what many spiritual teachers say. When you're in stillness, in the gap between thoughts, that's where you'll find your loving source. By finding time to go within, you're strengthening your connection to your inner power and loving coach. Be open to intuitive hits and messages.

Taking time to be still and do guided imagery may help you shift more into peace and well-being, especially if you're dealing with an illness or chronic condition yourself or with your child. You need a safe place to find relief. Today, we hunger for connection and meaning in our stressed-out world. It seems the more we celebrate technology, the more we feel disconnected. We manage long to-do lists, email, texting, and social media. But in the end, how is this supporting our quality of life?

Children pick up on stress and are very sensitive to their parents' emotions. If you're calm, your kids will sense that. And the opposite is also true—your stress and anxiety will be felt by your children and may affect their health and well-being. That's why I want to help you and your family find calm, peace, and healing together. Plus, as I had mentioned in my introduction, recent studies show that a regular practice by parents being more mindful can enhance your children's emotional wellbeing.

Let the whole family enjoy more peace and calm, especially during difficult times. These guided meditations are offered on top of the other imagery journeys for younger children that you are welcome to use, too. As a gentle reminder, Chapter 1 contains several breathing exercises, which are important for you to know and practice, as well. Plus, the next chapter has more mind-body tools to explore.

This chapter contains four imagery scripts. You're welcome to try them on your own or record them for your own use. These guided meditations are also available at InnerPowerMindset.com. They include:

- Stress Buster
- Evening Meditation: Letting Go
- Embrace Love Release Fear
- Blissful Sleep

Whether you're feeling overwhelmed and needing a break or want to start off your day in a better state, consider adding the *Stress Buster* guided imagery to your routine. This Guided Imagery gives you permission to let go of your worries, so you will feel stronger and be better able to cope with your life's challenges. Consider recording this meditation so you can relax fully while doing it. Just make sure to read it slowly and pause in between phrases to get the full relaxation effect.

Stress Buster for Parents and Teens

Find a quiet place where you will not be disturbed. Relax and get into a comfortable position, sitting up straight, with your hands in your lap facing up, or by your side if lying down. Now take 4 deep breaths in and out. As you breathe in, feel you are breathing in light and peace, and letting go of tension, stress, and negativity of the day. Remember to breathe in on a count of four: 1, 2, 3, 4…hold on a count of 4. (Pause briefly) Then release on a count of 4. Now take 3 more deep breaths. (Pause 20 seconds)

Continue to breathe lovingly, as you bring your awareness to the top of your head. Just sense or imagine a feeling of relaxation beginning to spread down from the top of your scalp. Like a warm, thick liquid melting away tension, feel the muscles in your forehead and temples relax. Allow your eye muscles to release. Let your cheeks and jaw soften, even your tongue. Let go of all tension with this soothing, warm, and relaxing energy.

Now let this peaceful feeling flow down into your neck. Feel it loosening every muscle and every fiber. This relaxation becomes deeper and warmer. With each breath, it travels deep into the muscles in your shoulders, soothing them and releasing all tension. Feel that your entire upper body has become loose, limp, and relaxed.

Feel this healing warmth flow into the rest of your body, releasing all tension and remaining pain as it flows down your legs and out through your feet. Your body feels heavier and looser. Relax more and more deeply with each breath. Sink into total serenity. As your body relaxes, your mind becomes more relaxed, and your thoughts seem to become lighter. You are slipping further into stillness and peace. (Pause 10 seconds)

Now imagine a place that makes you feel safe and at peace. It can be by an ocean in a tropical setting with beautiful palm trees and an emerald green sea. Or in a mountain setting with crystal white peaks and the smell of evergreen trees. Or choose a beautiful garden with lush flowers and trees.

Whatever place you choose will be just right for you. Imagine what it feels like. What sounds do you hear? What scents do you smell…being in your special place? What beauty do you see? Allow the feeling of getting away from it all to flood your body. Take in how this place makes you feel safe and serene. (Pause)

Now imagine finding a place to sit. You can choose anything you want…a hammock, a big soft chair, or even a blanket.

Let yourself rest in your space of love and healing. This is all about your peace, and you can come back to this place whenever you want to create more balance in your life. Living more at ease allows you to do the things you need to do in life much easier. (Pause briefly) You can still be responsible but with much less stress, with a calmer mind. Much less worry, much less fatigue… As you are learning to release tension, you feel more peace and calm. When your body is relaxed, and you respond to life with more ease, you have more energy to increase your health and happiness. (Pause briefly)

Being balanced, you are now more focused on your daily tasks but with a sense of serenity. You see things now with a clearer mind and increased confidence. This increased energy allows you to shift any negative thought or worry into a positive thought and feeling. (Pause briefly)

Know that as you work lovingly toward yourself, your sense of security and ease becomes stronger, more profound in its depth, being the truth of who you are—a powerful being. Now you feel grounded in accepting who you are on a whole new level of possibilities.

The more you act this way, the more confidence you have. You experience life in a more playful and balanced way. It feels good to feel positive; to expect the best from life and know that life supports you. You are grounded and let go of negative limitations. And you enjoy your healthy choices reaching your personal goals. In a conscious way and a feeling of "I can do it," you relax and make it happen.

See how good it feels reaching your goals… appreciating how you handle life now with grace and effortless flow. Welcome your deepest thoughts and heartfelt emotions and a knowing that all is well in your world. All tension that had been removed earlier from your body from your head to your toes… now see a new light of peace and serenity replacing that tension that comes up through your toes, your legs, lower body…into the center of your being, your back, your arms, shoulders, upper body, neck into your head and scalp…now filling up with total new energy, peace, and serenity.

So, as I count you back now… Feeling refreshed and energized from all that you received. I will bring you up…more aware now at 4…halfway there now at 3…take a deep breath at 2… feeling refreshed and alert now at 1. Come back into this room and, when you're ready, open your eyes.

While it's great to start your day with meditation, like my *Morning Light Meditation* in Chapter 3, it can be just as enriching to end your day with meditation and to let go… to let go of any worry and stress you accumulated during the day. Best-selling author, the late Wayne Dyer in *Wishes Fulfilled*, talked about the last five minutes before you fall asleep as being the most important to your well-being and for manifesting your desires. What you plant in your mind is what your subconscious will repeat during the next eight hours of sleep.[19] If you're focused on all that went wrong and your worries, that's what your subconscious will stir up overnight. Begin to plant statements like "I am well," or "I am safe," or "I am loved." Think about your blessings. Those are the positive messages you want to send to your subconscious at night. This next imagery is best to use at the end of your day or at bedtime.

Evening Meditation: Letting Go

Find a quiet spot where you will not be disturbed. Relax and get into a comfortable position, sitting up straight, with your hands in your lap or, if you're lying down, hands by your sides. Now take 4 deep breaths in and out. We're going to be "Breathing Like a Navy SEAL for Calm and Focus," or the Boxed Breath. Now, if breathing in on a count of four is too difficult, you may breathe in on the count of 3 or 2. So let's begin. First breathe out.

Now breathe in on a count of 4, 1, 2, 3, 4, hold on a count of 4 (Pause briefly) then release on a count of 4. (Pause.) And Pause for four. (Pause.) Continue breathing like this for a few moments. (Pause for 20 seconds.)

As you breathe in, feel you are breathing in light and peace, and letting go of any tension, stress, and negativity of the day. Continue to breathe lovingly, as you bring your awareness to the top of your head. Just sense or imagine a feeling of relaxation beginning to spread down from the top of your scalp like a warm, thick liquid melting away tension throughout your body.

This nurturing warmth releases all tension and any pain. Your body feels heavier and heavier. Relax more and more deeply with each breath. Sink into total serenity. As your body relaxes, your mind becomes more relaxed, and your thoughts seem to become lighter. You are slipping further into stillness and peace. Notice how good it feels to be so gently embraced.

Feel a glowing light become so large, that it wraps you in a beautiful cocoon of protective light...providing you with total peace, safety, and love. Now I want you to imagine in your mind's eye that you are going down a set of 5 steps. With each step you are doubling your relaxation...from 5 to 4, releasing further, 3 going deeper and deeper...to 2, now down to 1... totally relaxed and at peace. (Pause briefly)

Let yourself go to the most serene place that you can imagine—a place of peace and safety, like by an ocean or mountainside. (Pause 5 seconds) Go to this beautiful place that makes you feel calm. (Pause 30 seconds) Let yourself breathe in this beautiful, safe place. You can go to this place at any time. It's a place full of wisdom and total serenity.

Feel your heart open just a little bit more... a warm expansion of healing energy. Feel grateful for this place of healing and peace. (Pause briefly) And now it's time...to become aware of a loving presence, pure awareness of source energy. Just be in the stillness of space feeling surrounded by unconditional love. (Pause 30 seconds)

Now bring to mind any successes from this past day. Reflect on the big and the small ones. Stay with this for a few moments. (Pause 1 minute) With compassion, ask your inner coach to reflect on what you could have done better. (Pause 30 seconds) Now bring in love and compassion and let the day go.

Take a moment to think about your day tomorrow. Picture it going exactly the way you want it to go. Also, include any positive habits that you will complete. (Pause 30 seconds) In your mind's eye, picture them already accomplished with grace and ease.

Now place your hand over your heart. Thank your body, your mind, and the Divine for inspiring you to greatness. For gratitude is the ultimate state of receiving. Feel this appreciation now. (Pause 20 seconds)

Welcome your deepest thoughts and heartfelt emotions and a knowing that all is well in your world. (Pause 10 seconds) Feel the love surrounding you in a blanket of peace. (Pause 20 seconds) If you are listening to this at night, intending to sleep, just drift off into a deep, restful sleep until morning, and ignore the next statement. If it is time for you to be awake… take two deep breaths. Feel yourself come back into the room and when you are ready, open your eyes.

The next guided imagery will reduce anxiety and stress by helping you fall into a deep state of relaxation. In this state, you'll feel unconditional love and be able to release all troubles and burdens by giving your problems to a loving source and a higher power to handle. By reducing your concerns, you're empowered to plant the seeds necessary to create the life you want to live.

There's a wonderful book called *Love is Letting Go of Fear*, by Jerry Jampolsky. The book points out that we are either feeling love or fear. When we're in fear, we tend to view the world as unsafe, or that it's out to get us. Being in this attack mode, our thoughts tend to judge and criticize. The opposite is also true. Have you ever noticed when you feel love and are thankful, the universe seems to be conspiring for your good? When you're in this loving state, you feel more gratitude and appreciate blessings. This guided imagery will help you return to love to release fear and anxiety.

Embrace Love, Release Fear

Make your body comfortable. Uncross your arms and legs and relax in your chair with your eyes closed. Or, you may find a spot on the wall or on the floor. We're going to breathe in and out on a count of 4. If this is too difficult, you may breathe in and out on the count of 3 or 2. So let's begin. First breathe out. Now breathe in on a count of 4... 1, 2, 3, 4... hold for 4... then breath out for 4. (Pause 4 seconds) And Pause for four. Do this a few more times... (Pause 20 seconds.)

Now let go of counting and breathe normally. Now see a beautiful white light from above. It bathes the top of your head and flows into your scalp and down into your neck. Just release all tension with this white light. As the beautiful light travels through your body, see your shoulders totally let go, and your arms and hands relax, too. As it moves into your back and core area, let all tension go. This soothing energy now flows into your hips, then legs, and on through to your feet. If there is any tension left, just send it down through your feet into the earth. You feel supported and grounded. Stay in this peaceful bliss for few moments. (Pause 30 seconds) Imagine there are five steps and as you go down each step, you are doubling your relaxation. 5, 4 keep doubling that relaxation. 3… more serene and letting go, 2, and now down to 1, on that bottom step. You're totally open to new ideas.

In your mind's eye, imagine a beautiful, safe place that brings you comfort and peace, perhaps by the sea… Imagine this beautiful aqua blue ocean… safe and serene. Or it can be by a mountainside. Feel the sun on your body, hear the waves, smell the air, breathe in this peaceful place for a few moments.… (Pause briefly) You can go to this place at any time. It's a place full of wisdom and total serenity. Stay here in this safe place for a few moments. (Pause for 30 seconds)

You now leave this safe place, for now, knowing you can return any time. As you breathe in and out, bring your awareness to the base of your spine, bless this energy center, and just let your body feel grounded and centered in this healing ball of light. Now move this healing energy up into your heart. Feel a beautiful golden divine light. At the same time, feel a beautiful divine golden light in from the top of your head that just pours down into your heart. Feel embraced by the divine helping you heal and transform. (Pause 30 seconds)

Now is the time to love yourself and release the past. Allow your heart to feel this magnificent healing warmth and unconditional love. (Pause 20 seconds)

With gratitude, know that this loving energy is here to support you, allow yourself to release all your burdens to your creator. Just give your problems to your higher power or higher self. Total surrender as you feel love's peace.

Any fear that is left in your body, any pain that is in any part of your body, release it all. Ask your higher power for help and guidance. And I will be quiet for a few moments. (Pause 30)

Where there's fear, let there be love. Where there is doubt, let there be courage. Feel this beautiful love filling up your being. Trust a higher source for answers. (Pause 20 seconds)

Say to yourself but not out loud

- *I release all my fears to my higher self. (Pause briefly)*
- *I let go, forgive, and trust that life will bring my heart's desires. (Pause briefly)*
- *I surrender all pain and let love fill up my entire mind and body with peace.*

So now imagine your life a few months from now. You're in charge and creating the life you desire. All you need to do is let go and feel grounded and supported. With gratitude, place your hand over your heart. Thank a higher power for this wonderful life. Review in your mind how you will move forward taking all of this radiance within you, letting your healthy light shine. Let go with ease and confidence in creating your best life. (Pause for 10 seconds)

So now it's time to return where we began. Welcome your deepest thoughts and heartfelt emotions and a knowing that all is well in your world. So, now as I count you back ... Feeling refreshed and energized from all that you received. I will bring you up ... from 4...halfway there now at 3...take a deep breath at 2... feeling refreshed and alert now at 1. Come back into this room and when you're ready, open your eyes.

Managing Stress

Releasing stress and anxiety are important to do on a regular basis for your peace and well-being. Too much worry can impact sleep. According to the Centers for Disease Control (CDC), nearly 35 percent of adults–one in three adults suffer from regular insomnia.[20]

Guided Imagery can help relax the mind and body allowing us to let go of worries and fall asleep more quickly. The next healing meditation is for sleep. The more you listen to this mediation, the easier it will be to fall and stay asleep. One study found that worrying about not getting enough sleep may cause more anxiety and problems.[21] We may do better if we remember to trust that our inner being knows how to fall asleep and remain at rest. In the following meditation, I plant this reminder into your deeper subconscious.

If you have trouble with sleep and insomnia, set up a more conducive bedtime ritual. Stay away from electronics and your smartphone an hour or more before bed. Take a warm bath or shower. Listen to soft music or those sound machines with soothing sounds. Maybe keep a worry notebook by your bed in which you write down thoughts that may keep you up so you can let them go. *Blissful Sleep* will help relax your mind and body to enjoy a more restorative sleep. For best results, use the audio program available on our website.

Blissful Sleep for Adults and Teens

Take a moment to make sure that you are in a comfortable spot away from anything that could disturb you. For this is your time to relax and restore. Get comfortable now. Lie down on your bed or another surface, with your arms at your sides. Please close your eyes and go inside. Just let go for now.

First, let's focus on your breathing. I want you to breathe in a special way. You begin to relax tension as you breathe in on the count of 4....1, 2, 3, 4...hold for 4, then release tension 1, 2, 3, 4. And pause for four. Once more, breathe in on a count of 4… pause for 4…release for 4… and pause once more. Keep breathing like that for a few moments. (Pause for 20 seconds.) It's so good to know that by noticing the rise and fall of your chest that you are well on your way to relaxation and sleep.

Continue breathing in and out lovingly and you no longer need to count. As you release all tension in your mind and body, second by second, moment by moment, you will find that you will free yourself from any thoughts of stress and worry of the day. Just let it all go for this peaceful time for you. (Pause 10 seconds)

Now, let yourself imagine a healing ball of light…that is just above your head. (Pause 5 seconds) Let this healing light flow into your body, beginning at the top of your head. Feel a soothing warm wave of relaxation beginning at the top of your scalp, and spreading downwards, melting away all tension. Imagine a warm thick liquid releasing all stress. Let go of any tension around your eyes. Feel your eyelids become very heavy and very relaxed, more and more at peace. You will be surprised and amazed that with each breath, you are becoming more and more relaxed.

Your forehead is smooth and relaxed. Let go of any tension in your temples. Let your jaw relax by allowing your mouth to be slightly open and let your tongue relax. Just let go. Even your ears are becoming relaxed. Feel your throat release, loosen any tightness. Relax your cheeks and any muscles in your face. Continue this relaxation. Enjoy the peace and calm that you feel. (Pause 10 seconds)

Now let's focus on your neck. Allow that warm glow of relaxation, beginning at the top of your neck, flow down into your shoulders. How wonderful your body feels as it melts into total relaxation. Feel all tension release from your shoulders, becoming loose and limp, through your collarbone. Let your shoulders sink gently downward, as they feel heavy and very relaxed. Deeper and deeper into total peace and relaxation.

Turn your attention to both arms. Feel the relaxation flowing down your shoulders and allow your upper arms to relax, feel the warm liquid energy flow down into your elbows, forearms, even your wrists. They feel heavy and are sinking deeper. They become totally loose and limp, all the way down into your fingertips. Release and let go. (Pause 10 seconds)

Bring your awareness now to the center of your being around your navel. Feel how this area of your body and chest gently rises and falls as you breathe. This peaceful sensation flows throughout this area of your body, soothing every muscle and relaxing every organ. You can feel the release, as all muscles go limp and heavy, sinking deeper and deeper. (Pause 10 seconds)

Focus on your upper back. Feel the warm thick liquid of relaxation flow down your spine. Let all the muscles surrounding each vertebra become totally loose and limp. Release any tension in your upper back, middle and lower back. Enjoy this luxurious feeling of complete relaxation. Everything is melting away, only the peace of deep relaxation remains. (Pause 10 seconds)

Spread this relaxation through the lower part of your body. Release any tension and notice the calm and heavy relaxation in your hips. Feel this relaxation flow into your legs, calves, ankles, and feet, all the way into your toes. All that remains is deep healing and peaceful relaxation all throughout your body. You feel rooted and grounded. Isn't it good to know that every cell in your body feels total peace and serenity? Just release and let go. (Pause 20 seconds)

As you feel yourself becoming more physically relaxed, notice that you are becoming more mentally relaxed. Let go of any remaining thoughts—thoughts that no longer need to be there. You'll soon be counting backgrounds in your mind's eye, doubling your mental relaxation. As you slowly count backwards from 100, you'll notice that the numbers disappear and float away. So, by the time you get to the number 97 or even sooner, your mind will be so relaxed, all thoughts will drift away. Begin counting: 100, 99, 98...97 (Pause 10 seconds) Excellent.... Keep counting as the numbers fade away... (Pause 5 seconds)

Now I want you to imagine walking down a small, heavenly staircase. (Pause 5 seconds) This stairway to dreams leads down to a beautiful soft cloud of comfort and rest. (Pause 5 seconds) As you take your first step...5. (Pause briefly) Your mind is relaxed as your body is relaxed, your mind and body are doubling in relaxation. (Pause briefly) Going down to 4. More and more deeply relaxed, more and more connected to that inner awareness that knows exactly how to help you with any issue. (Pause briefly) 3...going deeper and deeper into total relaxation. 2...This stepping stone for your continued progress and serenity (Pause briefly) and 1...now you're on the bottom step more and more deeply relaxed and completely open and receptive. As you step off, it's like you're resting on a beautiful cloud, like a soft blanket so comforting and serene. Just float away...as you soak up these ideas. (Pause 10 seconds)

Feel total peace and serenity. Feel deeply relaxed just where you are and continue breathing in and out slowly. With each breath, the wisdom of your mind-body knows exactly how to fall and stay asleep. You now move into a restorative sleep knowing it's time for beautiful renewal and rest. Just let go and let it happen. Feel surrounded by comfort and peace. Know you will dream wonderful, healing dreams. (Pause for 10.) If you should awaken before it's time to be up, just say to yourself "Blissful Sleep," and you will return to a deep relaxing sleep. (Pause 20 seconds)

In your mind's eye imagine a beautiful warm shower of soft healing rain that bathes your entire head and body. (Pause 5 seconds) Notice how these droplets carry a healing message for all the cells in your body—to relax, restore and sleep. (Pause 5 seconds) Feel this shower of light rain wash over your entire being. Absorb this beautiful healing energy throughout your entire body. Stay here for a few moments, enjoying it all. (Pause 20 seconds)

Feel a warm towel soaking up any remaining water as you lie down and relax in your surroundings… totally refreshed by the healing water that bathed every cell of your body. Now you cover your body with a warm, luscious blanket that surrounds you with unconditional love. Feel safe and protected….

Now imagine a white light beginning in your core or center of your body, around your navel. And see it grow and expand into your heart and into your head, and throughout your entire body. Feel yourself bathing in this pool of white light that surrounds you now. This pool of white light is peaceful, loving and calm. You open up just a little bit more to allow in a deeper peace. Surrender and let go. Rest in this pure healing light. This healing energy is just for you and knows exactly where to go to heal your mind, body, and spirit. You will be surprised and amazed at how tranquil sleep transforms your body mind and spirit. Feel embraced by this peaceful, blissful sleep. (Pause 20 seconds)

Your body knows exactly what to do to allow your mind, body, and spirit to sleep peacefully. Let yourself drift into a beautiful, restorative sleep. Know that all is well in your world. As you continue to listen to this program, each time, it will help you fall and stay asleep more easily. Feel surrounded by a beautiful healing energy that soothes and restores every cell in your body. Isn't it good to know that you are returning to your natural ability to reach a wonderful, warm and restorative sleep? (Pause 10 seconds) Enjoy this dreamy feeling of blissful sleep.

Rest is so crucial for our well-being to nourish and rejuvenate our mind and body. This guided imagery program and many more are available through our companion website. You may also use *Blissful Sleep* if you wake up in the middle of the night. It will help you fall back to sleep.

Besides guided imagery, there are a few breathing exercises that may also help you relax and calm your thoughts for rest. Remember the breathing technique *Sixteen Seconds to Bliss* or the *Box Breath*. (Chapter 1) I use this when I have trouble falling asleep. As you may recall, you breathe in on a count of four seconds, hold for four, breathe out on a count of four, and then pause for four. Somehow, the pause in the breathing helps us relax much more quickly. Another option is to use this powerful mantra: "I am loved, I am safe, I am at peace" until you fall back to sleep. It's the same phrase I use in *Sleepytime Dreams* for children. It's just as soothing for adults.

Wishing you sweet dreams and better sleep! In the next chapter, please enjoy more mindful practices and mind-body tools. They will boost your health and happiness!

CHAPTER 11

Your Healing Journey Continues

If you've come to this chapter, this is not the end, but the beginning. You and your child or teen will continue this journey together for more peace and healing. Thank you for allowing me into your hearts and minds. For that, I am so grateful. You hold the power, as I had mentioned earlier in this book. Use these mindful exercises and imagery scripts and my recordings to help you tap into your inner light for strength.

We are mostly made of energy. Yet, we think we're just our physical body. This beautiful energy and inner light connects us to the light source above and below. It can be brought in for healing and comfort. That's where your SUPERPOWER within connects you to love and a higher source.

Additional Mind-Body Tools and Techniques

While the majority of my book has dealt with various types of meditation, guided imagery scripts, and stories, several mindfulness techniques can also be helpful. These practices can help you focus on the present moment, raise your awareness and focus, as well as heal pain and suffering. The parents at a pediatric hospital have found these to be helpful. Here are a few of my favorites that may be beneficial to you, as well. I'm also including a mind-body technique known as Emotional Freedom Technique (EFT) or Meridian Tapping that's helpful in releasing stress, pain, and emotional blocks.

STOP One-Minute Breathing and Mindfulness Exercise

Here's a helpful one-minute mindfulness practice that can bring us to the present moment and diminish our worry or negative thinking. I meet so many people who feel like there's too much to do, not enough time, and that they're in a constant state of stress. Others are facing tough medical decisions and the fear of the unknown. When we're in stress-mode, it's hard to think clearly or see any situation accurately. In this state, it's hard to be our best selves.

With practice, we may turn to the STOP One-Minute Breath when feeling stressed out, angry, or just needing a break in our day. This mindfulness exercise will help you shift from being reactive and fearful to pausing before possibly overreacting. It's a tool that will help you build your mental fitness that you can use at any time.

- **S: Stop.** *Whenever you notice stress or imbalance, pause and become aware of the present moment. Tune in to see if you feel stressed or out-of-balanced.*

- **T: Take a breath**. *Bring your awareness to your body. Notice your breathing by taking a few slow calming breaths. Also, notice how your mind begins to settle. Calm breathing will turn off the "fight or flight" part of the brain.*

- **O: Observe**. Feel how the breath begins to open your heart and mind naturally. Let yourself just "be" in the moment. Be the observer; look around to see what's happening around you. Find three things to see and then three things to hear. Feel free to bring in other senses, too.

- **P: Proceed**. Having shifted to a more mindful presence, you may move forward and proceed. You'll probably have a more creative and better way to handle the situation.

The more we practice this mindfulness technique, the less we'll overreact or let stress get the best of us. Whenever possible, remember this STOP one-minute breathing exercise. Allow your inner coach and observer to stand back and help you make wiser choices. As bestselling author Victor Frankl once said, "Between stimulus and response there is a space. In that space is our power to choose our response. In our response lies our growth and our freedom." This exercise is a useful tool for experiencing more freedom and has been adopted by the Mindfulness-Based Stress Reduction program. [22]

Releasing Emotional Pain through Compassion

You may release pain and suffering by locating the seeds of your pain through a powerful mindfulness practice that I call the "Compassionate Freedom Technique." Instead of running from feelings or escaping in the usual ways, experiment with this technique to manage painful emotions or wounds. Show kindness toward the pain, allow in the feeling. Allow it to be held and nurtured and it will dissolve and go away more quickly.

After coaching a group of new moms at a pediatric hospital with this mindfulness exercise, one of them told me how useful it was for her. She encouraged me to use this exercise with high school students, so they could learn how to deal with pain and suffering in a constructive way, rather than escaping through drugs as she did with heroin. Because of her suggestion, I include this Compassion Freedom exercise whenever I train teachers, parents, and teens. I hope you find it beneficial, as well.

Compassion Freedom Technique

Think about a situation that is upsetting to you. Instead of distracting yourself from the feeling—like with alcohol or pain killers—be present to the physical sensation of this feeling in your body. Let go of your thoughts and focus on the body. Notice where in your body the feeling is the strongest. You may feel tightness in your stomach, throat, or chest. Discomfort could be located in other spots, as well. This Compassion Freedom Technique will help you release the pain.

- ***Step 1: Be Accepting and Soothing:*** *Close your eyes and slowly breathe in and out. Pause for 20 seconds.) Locate where you are feeling tightness or in pain. Bring comfort and compassion to that area of your body. (Pause 20 seconds.) Take a couple of deep cleansing breaths in and out. Let it wash over the pain.*

- ***Step 2: Find the Center of Pain****: This tough feeling is trying to get your attention, so be accepting and soothing toward it. Focus on your body where the feeling has the greatest intensity. (Pause.) With your attention on the pain, stay present to it in a loving way. As you give this feeling attention, soothing it like a baby, puppy, or dear friend, the intensity may shift to another area of the body. The feeling may become more or less intense. Keep staying with it. (Pause 20 seconds.) Once more, take a couple of deep cleansing breaths in and out. Let it wash over the pain.*

- ***Step 3: Bring Yourself Back to Calm****: Let it live, be accepting, and allow. Keep your attention on the most intense part of the pain in a loving way. You may also surround the feeling with a tiny healing waterfall to gently release the pain. That's it. Let the healing water soothe the pain. Most people begin to feel better after five or ten minutes. Keep repeating these three steps until the painful feelings subside. Sometimes difficult feelings or old wounds may take a few sessions to release.*

After the feeling has run its course, you'll be left with a neutral feeling. You may also be filled with more peace. To make sure that you've cleared the emotion from your body, recall the problem that was bothering you. Notice if you feel anything other than being calm or neutral about it. Sometimes several layers of pain need to be processed. You may have to soothe this painful issue several times. Freedom through self-compassion can help you deal with the realities of being human, which can mean you suffer at times. But now you have a better way to release pain and hurt while building emotional resilience.

I first practiced a similar technique at a mindfulness retreat. My experience was quite powerful. I was amazed at how pain was released rather quickly, and I felt so much better. This practice has been very beneficial to me and I hope it will be helpful to you, too.

Emotional Freedom Technique (EFT) Meridian Tapping

Emotional Freedom Technique (EFT) or Meridian Tapping is a great stress and pain reliever, and negative belief buster. This mind-body tool has been around for several decades, but in the last five years, EFT has become more mainstream. Life coaches and therapists now teach this technique to their clients because it works quickly. Even professional sports teams are using it. In fact, I know an energy psychologist who has been training professional sports players in these methods for pain control, anxiety, and game-day jitters. It may also be helpful for veterans with post-traumatic stress disorder (PTSD). Recent studies show that tapping can be effective along with other mind-body therapies.[23]

Emotional Freedom Technique was discovered by psychologist Roger Callahan in the early 1990s as a useful tool for panic attacks and anxiety. It's based on Chinese medicine and the meridian energy system and uses acupressure. Later, Gary

Craig worked with Callahan to simplify the tapping points, which made it easier to become more widely accepted.

Once you get the hang of EFT, you can do it on your own. However, if you've experienced trauma or abuse, you may want to work with a professional who's trained in these methods.

Sample Tapping Session

I've included a sample tapping script and a chart of the meridian points. Tapping can feel a little awkward at first because you're voicing your problems and pain out loud. Most of us aren't used to doing this, but stating your problem as you tap on the meridian points is how you release stress and pain from the body. As your stress levels and pain go down, you add in more empowering statements while continuing to tap. In the last round, you use only positive statements. Most people feel an energy shift after doing a ten-to-fifteen-minute session. Many websites, including ours have a demonstration video to watch and practice with. This is included in your special gift at InnerPowerMindset.com/IPNgift

Please see the Meridian Tapping Illustration chart to help you locate the various tapping points.

Illustration of Meridian Tapping Points Emotional Freedom Technique (EFT)

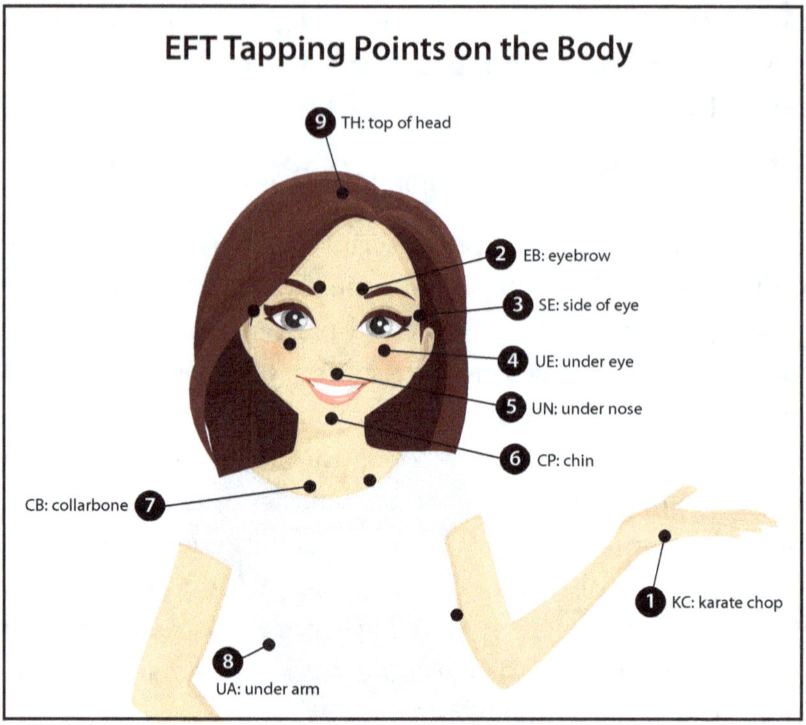

EFT Tapping Points on the Body

9 TH: top of head
2 EB: eyebrow
3 SE: side of eye
4 UE: under eye
5 UN: under nose
6 CP: chin
7 CB: collarbone
1 KC: karate chop
8 UA: under arm

© 2019 Vicki Atlas Israel and Inner Power Mindset

Script to Tap Away Stress with EFT

To begin this brief tapping session on stress, imagine something that recently occurred that has really stressed you out or is causing you pain. Now ask yourself, on a scale of 1 to 10, with 10 being the most stressed, how stressed are you right now? This number is called your "Subjective Units of Distress Scale" or SUDS." It's the number you gauge your stress level intensity against as you tap through each round. Tapping begins with a setup statement that includes the problem and a phrase of acceptance. For example, "Even though I have all of this stress and anxiety, I deeply and completely accept myself."

You'll begin by tapping on the Karate chop point 5 to 7 times. As you tap, say your setup statement three times before moving on to the other points. Tap gently, yet firmly, with the tips of two or three fingers. It's not meant to hurt or give you a headache, so take it easy. I will pause, so you will repeat the statements out loud that I say, as you continue tapping.

- **Karate Chop:** *Even though I feel stressed and overwhelmed, I deeply and completely accept myself.*

- **Karate Chop:** *Even though I'm stressed out because there's too much pressure, I chose to accept myself.*

- **Karate Chop:** *Even though I feel really stressed and anxious, I deeply and completely accept myself.*

After saying the setup statement three times, start going through the different meridian points from the chart. You'll be tapping 5 to 7 times on each point before moving to the next one. Again, use the tips of two or three fingers on each point with one hand. Say each phrase out loud.

- **Eyebrow:** Too much stress.
- **Side of Eye:** I feel overwhelmed.
- **Under Eye:** I'm so tense and can't let go.
- **Under Nose:** Too much to do and not enough time.
- **Above Chin:** I'm too stressed, too much pressure.
- **Collarbone:** Why are things so tough right now?
- **Under Arm:** I need to let go.
- **Top of Head:** But it's hard with all of this worry.

(Now continue moving through the points again.)

- **Eyebrow:** Why does life seem so hard?
- **Side of Eye:** What to do? I'm so upset.
- **Under Eye:** Can I choose to see this differently?
- **Under Nose:** No, I'm too stressed.
- **Above Chin:** What if I could breathe more calmly?
- **Collarbone:** But I feel too stressed. When will I feel better?
- **Under Arm:** Keep tapping and letting go.
- **Top of Head:** And remind me that all will be well in the end.

Now, take a deep breath . . . then let it go. Take another breath . . . and release. How do you feel? Did your stress go down at all? How would you rate your stress level now (1 to 10 scale with 10 being the highest) on SUDS? If there's something specific that's still upsetting you, continue tapping.

Remember, the more specific you can be on your issue the better. Tap for a final five minutes to release your stress, anxiety, or worry.

Keep the tapping illustration handy to continue using this helpful stress and pain reliever and please watch our video demo. Once you get the hang of it, you can teach this technique to younger children, so they can also benefit from EFT. Since kids also face stress, school pressures, and bullying, they may find this tool helpful. I've discovered that combining EFT with guided imagery is a potent mixture. Tapping first seems to release the old blocks or negativity, enabling you to go deeper with guided imagery to connect with something higher for answers.

With or without Tapping, continue using your imagination (mental imagery) for healing and comfort, surrendering to something higher for comfort and guidance. Remember that you can have a multisensory experience by going to our website and listening to the guided imagery recordings. You may also do imagery on your own. Here's a way to practice doing a visualization.

Visualize Your Goal

Try this brief imagery on your own for a few minutes. Choose one goal that you really want to accomplish, and set that as your intention. Whether it's for more healing and peace, better health, better relationships, or more success, you can create one as your goal. Here are the next steps to follow:

- Close your eyes and breathe deeply for several minutes, letting yourself unwind into a deeper state.
- Let all the tension out of your body for a minute or so.
- Then, connect to the light source from above and within your heart. Feel embraced by pure love for a few moments. Stay here for a minute or so in gratitude.
- Set your big intention. What do you most want to create as a dream or goal?
- Visualize yourself as that future self now in full living color, as vibrant as possible.
- As you imagine, remember to include all of your senses.
- Remember to add feelings of excitement and pride for what it will feel like when you reach your big goal.
- Once you have this feeling for one minute or more, put your hand on your heart in gratitude.
- Then let it go, and know that it is done. Do not become attached to a specific outcome. Release it to a Divine, Universal Power that knows how to create what is best for you.

Do this on a regular basis for thirty days or more on that one goal and see what may manifest. I believe this is how I attracted my husband into my life, and we've been married for over thirty years. This was my first real experience in the power of guided imagery or creative visualization. I was instructed to write what I most wanted in a relationship on a sheet of paper. At least two times per day, I closed my eyes and imagined this person coming into my life in vivid detail and with much enthusiasm. Two months later, I met my future husband at a personal growth conference. We became friends and a relationship developed a bit later. It was after we'd been dating for a month that I realized Jim had all of the main relationship qualities I'd written on my list!

Now, here I am thirty years later teaching you what I had experienced decades ago but lost for a while. I rekindled the gift of imagery and meditation when my stress and lack of sleep became problematic and was causing issues in my life. While I have studied and received certification, please know that you have access to this same phenomenal power.

Be ready and open for possible miracles. Keep using the power of imagery and opening your heart to co-create your soul's desires and to enjoy more peace and well-being for you and your children. There's a saying that is often used at the end of a yoga class. It's the word "Namaste," meaning the Spirit in me sees and acknowledges the Spirit in you. We are one. Within you is a divine spark connected to a higher intelligence. Allow your brilliant light to shine. For you are Spirit and Spirit is you!

Namaste!

Special Note to *Inner Power NOW* Readers

Dear Friends,

Please stay in touch as I want to hear about your successes! In fact, if you find something that works especially well, please share your story. Your suggestions may help others. If you have an idea for a healing journey, please share and send to me. We can then pay it forward so ALL may benefit.

As my gift, remember to log onto my website at **InnerPowerMindset.com/IPNgift** to receive your special gift along with my thanks for buying and reading my book. Let's keep expanding and creating together and sharing best practices for ourselves and for our children's health and happiness.

Your peace and healing is what drives me to deliver the best results. I'm always creating and would love for you to join my Inner Power Circle and Mastermind Group by going to my website or VickiAtlas.com. Plus, you'll receive our newsletter and access to powerful programs and events. My commitment remains to you and your family for learning and helping you thrive. Also, please consider writing a review. These can be so helpful to others.

Wishing you and your children peace and blessings!

Warmly,
Vicki

Vicki Atlas-Israel, CGIP
Author | Speaker | Best Mindset Coach
Certified Guided Imagery Practitioner
Media Specialist
Vicki@InnerPowerMindset.com
www.InnerPowerMindset.com

Acknowledgments

Thank you to all who have contributed to my life, this book, and my journey. I am grateful to the beautiful clients and families that I have worked with in private practice and at the pediatric hospital. You enrich my life by being YOU.

I am so deeply thankful to New York Times Bestselling Author Jack Canfield, co-creator of *Chicken Soup for the Soul Series*® and *The Success Principles*®. Jack offered to endorse my book at his *Breakthrough to Success* Conference in front of hundreds of people. That divine moment has inspired me to finish this book. Jack, your generosity and belief in my efforts have rocked my world.

I am grateful to my loving husband Jim Israel, my partner and soul-mate, who has helped make this book possible. I appreciate your love and amazing support to help me launch this dream. You have spent countless hours on this book, programs, and offered wonderful guidance. To my sons, Andrew Israel and Jonathan Israel, I appreciate your encouragement. You are both amazing with many talents and gifts, and I am proud to be your mom.

Each one of my sisters is so special to me for their loving support. To my sister Laurie Schlesinger, thank you for your beautiful giving spirit and encouragement, and for Brother-in-Law Howard Schlesinger, my legal advisor. You both are greatly appreciated. I'm grateful to my sister Marilyn Atlas Needham and her husband Scott Needham who have encouraged and supported my work in meditation and guided imagery. As a licensed Social Worker and Hypnotherapist, Marilyn has inspired my guided imagery scripts. Thank you to my sister Patti Howe, who has motivated my work with children. As a child development specialist, Patti also reviewed my book, giving helpful insight.

Thank you to cousins Al and Nancy Malnik, who are the first contributors to *Inner Power NOW*, and to my dream of helping families and children through my book and programs. Special thanks also to my wonderful extended family in St. Louis and around the country, as well as those who are no longer living. You are forever in my heart! I especially want to honor Lucille Krachmalnick. My character "Lucy the Llama" is named after my Aunt Lucille, who always made each of us feel so loved and special.

I am also so deeply grateful to the following endorsements:

Anita Moorjani, Author of *Dying to Be Me* and *What If This Is Heaven*. Your amazing near-death experience and what you returned to teach has been miraculous! Your beautiful spirit and words continue to inspire us on how to better treat illness with more love and caring and "to live fearlessly."

James Baraz, Mindfulness Teacher and Author of *Awakening Joy*. Your calm ways and beautiful words have always encouraged me to model your way of peace and presence. Only through your care would I have attempted a silent mindfulness retreat.

Sandy Jost, Mentor, Guided Imagery Coach, Author, and friend. You continue to inspire my journey into this field of Holistic Healing. Your teachings and guidance have made a big contribution to my work. Thank you for also being an early reviewer of my book, guided imagery, and supporting my dreams.

Judy Fischer-Sadoff, beautiful client and mother of Hana, who offered such a wonderful heart-felt endorsement of my book. I am so honored to have worked with you and your family and to have brought a little peace during a difficult life transition. You and your daughter Hana will always be very special to me.

To my dear friends, the *Lovelies Mastermind Group*, Catharine Magel, Yvonne Schwandt, Michele Magner, and Sandy Tomey. You have sparked my journey and continue to support my dreams. To Catharine, my very talented artist and long-time friend, I love your beautiful illustrations of Lucy the Llama—so magical and lovable. As a child development specialist, Michele also helped by being an early reviewer of my book. Both Yvonne and Sandy have encouraged and offered wonderful coaching and upliftment.

There have been so many others who have helped bring this book to life. I'm grateful to Cathy and Jack Davis who are my Indie Book Coaches and Designers of my amazing book cover and branding. Cathy, you've been a wonderful coach in helping me publish this book, and Jack thank you for making my book sparkle on the inside. Special thanks to my editor Lisbeth Tanz, who has honored my words and spirit in this book to make it flow even better. Thanks also to proofreader Marianne Meeder.

Special thanks to my talented friend and Motion Graphics Editor Cheryl Anderson and Videographer Jason Metropoulos for your beautiful work. Also, thanks to Web Designer Korin Iverson Amin for the book's website.

I am also very grateful to my mentors: Steve Epner and Cynthia Correll for being advisors and dream-makers. Also included are Karen Hoffman, Keith Grosz, Gary Deeken, and Ken Herold. Thanks to my *Breakthrough to Success* Mastermind Group: Christine Bruce, Lindsay Gledhill, and Alp Isin for accountability, and to my BTS Writer's Group. I also want to thank Susan Scribner, Kathy Bernard, Lisa Collier, Gypsy Pate and others for being great cohorts in the *Prosper Women Mastermind Group*. (Now *Brazen Global.*)

To all of my early reviewers, thank you for taking time to offer your honest feedback of *Inner Power NOW*. I'm deeply grateful for your help and friendship!

My last big thank you is to the many teachers, mentors, family, friends, colleagues, and clients over the years. You have enriched my life in numerous ways!

Endnotes

(1) R. Morgan Griffin, "10 Health Problems Related to Stress That You Can Fix", https://www.webmd.com/balance/stress-management/features/10-fixable-stress-related-health-problems#1, accessed December 29, 2017

(2) Sara Whitney Lazar, "Defining and Measuring Mindfulness," Harvard University https://connects.catalyst.harvard.edu/Profiles/display/Person/12961, accessed September 17, 2017

(3) Thomas M. Ball, Daniel E.Shapiro, Cynthia Monheim, "A Pilot Study of the Use Of Guided Imagery for the Treatment of Recurrent Abdominal Pain in Children," http://journals.sagepub.com/doi/abs/10.1177/000992280304200607 , accessed October 14, 2017

(4) Jaswinder Ghuman, Hariwinder Ghuman, "ADHD in Preschool Children: Assessment and Treatment" Oxford University Press, 2014, Page 193

(5) Merriam-Webster's Dictionary, www.Merriam-Webster.com, Definition Mindfulness, accessed September 17, 2017

(6) Mark Divine, The Breathing Technique a Navy SEAL Uses to Stay Calm and Focused, (May 6, 2016)   http://time.com/author/mark-divine/, accessed April 10, 2018

(7) Cleveland Clinic, "Don't Believe Everything You Think," http://www.clevelandclinicwellness.com/programs/NewSFN/pages/default.aspx?Lesson=3&Topic=1&UserId=00000000-0000-0000-0000-000000000705, accessed January 28, 2018

(8) Lynne Shallcross, "Parents Can Learn How to Prevent Anxiety in Their Children," https://www.npr.org/sections/health-shots/2015/09/25/443444964/parents-can-learn-how-to-prevent-anxiety-in-their-children, accessed September 20, 2017

(9) Masaru Emoto, "What is the Photograph of Frozen Water Crystals" accessed March 28, 2018. http://www.masaru-emoto.net/english/water-crystal.html

(10) Scientific American https://www.scientificamerican.com/article/what-is-the-function-of-t-1997-12-22/

(11) Barbara L. Fredrickson, Michael A. Cohen, Kimberly A. Coffey, Open Hearts Build Lives: Positive Emotions Induced Through Loving-Kindness Meditation," https://www.ncbi.nlm.nih.gov/pmc/articles/PMC3156028/, accessed September 4, 2017

(12) Wayne Dyer, "Being in Balance," Hay House, Inc. Audio Book, USA (2006)

(13) Rollin McCraty, "The Energetic Heart: Bioelectromagnetic Communication Within and Between People, HeartMath Institute https://www.heartmath.org/research/research-library/energetics/energetic-heart-bioelectromagnetic-communication-within-and-between-people/, accessed December 29, 2017

(14) Robert Emmons, Thanks: How the New Science of Gratitude Can Make Your Happier, Hougton Mifflin Company, Boston-New York (2008)

(15) Bellaruth Naperstek, "Guided Imagery 101," http://www.healthjourneys.com/Main/Home/What-Is-Guided-Imagery/, accessed September 25, 2017

(16) Gay Hendricks, "How to Use Visualization to Heal Physically or Emotionally" https://www.gaiam.com/blogs/discover/how-to-use-visualization-to-heal-physically-or-emotionally, accessed September 15, 2017

(17) Deb Cheslow, The Connection Between Nasa and Habits: http://www.debcheslow.com/the-connection-between-nasa-and-habits/, accessed March 10, 2018

(18) Sophie Bethune, American Psychological Association Survey Shows Teen Stress Rivals that of adults, http://www.apa.org/news/press/releases/2014/02/teen-stress.aspx - page 23, accessed March 30, 2018

(19) Wayne Dyer, "Wishes Fulfilled: Mastering the Art of Manifesting," Hay House, Inc., Carlsbad, CA (2012), Page 157

(20) Centers for Disease Control and Prevention, "Getting Enough Sleep?" https://www.cdc.gov/features/getting-enough-sleep/index.html, accessed January 17, 2018

(21) Catharine Paddock, "Worrying About Insomnia May Cause More Harm than Poor Sleep." https://www.medicalnewstoday.com/articles/320025.php, accessed January 17, 2018

(22) Dave Potter, "STOP: The One-minute Breathing Space," https://palousemindfulness.com/MBSR/week4.html, accessed July 10, 2018

(23) Dawson Church, Audrey Brooks, "Effect of Emotional Freedom Techniques (EFT) on Psychological Trauma in Veterans, http://www.veteransefttappingproject.org/scientific-research-on-eft, accessed November 10, 2017

About the Author

Vicki Atlas Israel is on a mission to help children, teens, and families discover their inner power for stress relief and healing. As a Best Mindset Coach and Certified Guided Imagery Practitioner, Vicki's goal is to help families enjoy richer lives. As a consultant to a pediatric hospital and in her private practice, she coaches breathing techniques, meditation, and guided imagery that can reduce stress and pain and boost resilience. She helps coaching clients transform their lives and discover an inner healer and coach that will provide comfort, healing, and inspiration.

Vicki has been trained and is certified in Guided Imagery through ONE Health Academy for Integrative Medicine. Vicki has attended *Breakthrough to Success Training*, with New York Times Best-selling Author Jack Canfield, co-creator of *Chicken Soup for the Soul* Series® and *The Success Principles*®. Vicki been meditating daily for 10 years and has taken Progressive and Advanced Meditation Training with Dr. Joe Dispenza, Chiropractor, Speaker, and bestselling Author of *You*

Are the Placebo and *Becoming Supernatural.* She has been trained in mindfulness and attended mindfulness retreats with James Baraz, author of *Awakening Joy.* Outside of speaking and coaching, Vicki also enjoys singing, dancing, meditating, yoga, and having fun with family and friends. She lives in St. Louis, Missouri and is married with two adult sons.

Please see Vicki's website InnerPowerMindset.com that includes video and audio programs featured in this book.

www.ingramcontent.com/pod-product-compliance
Lightning Source LLC
Chambersburg PA
CBHW071203070526
44584CB00019B/2903